PREP. _. _. .

A Detailed Crises Plan for Living Comfortably
Through a Catastrophe

(Off-the-grid and Wilderness Preparedness)

Suzanne Kelly

Published by Martin Debroh

Suzanne Kelly

All Rights Reserved

Prepper: A Detailed Crises Plan for Living Comfortably Through a Catastrophe (Off-the-grid and Wilderness Preparedness)

ISBN 978-1-77485-102-9

Legal & Disclaimer

The information contained in this book is not designed to replace or take the place of any form of medicine or professional medical advice. The information in this book has been provided for educational and entertainment purposes only.

The information contained in this book has been compiled from sources deemed reliable, and it is accurate to the best of the Author's knowledge; however, the Author cannot guarantee its accuracy and validity and cannot be held liable for any errors or omissions. Changes are periodically made to this book. You must consult your doctor or get professional medical advice before using any of the suggested remedies, techniques, or information in this book.

Upon using the information contained in this book, you agree to hold harmless the Author from and against any damages, costs, and expenses, including any legal fees potentially resulting from the application of any of the information provided by this guide. This disclaimer applies to any damages or injury caused by the use and application, whether directly or indirectly, of any advice or information presented, whether for breach of contract, tort, negligence, personal injury, criminal intent, or under any other cause of action.

You agree to accept all risks of using the information presented inside this book. You need to consult a professional medical practitioner in order to ensure you are both able and healthy enough to participate in this program.

Table of Contents

Introduction

At one point in your life, you may have been told or even shared with others a piece of advice that runs along the lines of, "Stop being so negative! Stop letting those worst case scenarios play around in your head!" And while most of the time, these words are said with good intentions, the exact opposite and less popular opinion, however, might save your life instead: "Do think about the worst case scenario, and prepare ahead of time should it really come."

Just like the fable about the grasshopper who played all summer and died of hunger during the winter, and the ant that toiled and stocked up all summer, thus having enough to save its whole colony come winter, a family that prepares their pantry ahead of time will most likely survive an emergency situation should it come, like a storm, blizzard, power outage or even a zombie apocalypse.

Of course, preparing your emergency or survival pantry - as what many may call it – is not just simply buying food products and storing them in cupboards. There are may factors to consider and key points to remember in order to make your pantry a well-stocked emergency kitchen that can last the whole family two weeks or more.

This book will be your reliable, comprehensive guide to preparing your survival pantry. Grab a pen and jot down notes, if you must; your family will have you to thank for when the survival pantry saves everyone's lives.

Chapter 1: Why Should You Be A Prepper

You have probably heard a lot about the prepping movement that seems to be picking up steam. Do you know what it means to be a prepper? Should you join the movement and become a prepper? That is a pretty easy question to answer. Do you want to have the best chance at survival following a natural disaster, act of war or civil unrest? This is why people who are already prepping do what they do. We have seen what happens after a major event, like Hurricane Katrina or the massive earthquake in Haiti. Things get absolutely chaotic in the aftermath of a storm or other serious catastrophe. Anything that threatens our way of living has the ability to turn our world upside down. If we can't get to the store to get the things we need to live, it gets very serious very quick.

When you make the decision to prep, which is short for preparing, you are taking your life into your own hands. You are not going to sit around waiting for FEMA or some other government agency to come to your rescue. You are doing what is necessary to take care of your family's needs by stocking some key essentials that can mean the difference between life and death. Being prepared for anything gives you peace of mind and allows you to focus on your family rather than worrying about how you will find your next meal or where you will find clean water. Prepping means you have taken care of all of that and you only need to worry about keeping the family together and safe.

Some people scoff at the idea of prepping and take the position that nothing will ever happen or choose to just go with the flow of things if the world is turned upside down. Preppers often get a bad reputation and are ridiculed for being extreme. That is only one side of the prepping movement. There are plenty of "normal" people who choose to prep, without building intricate underground bunkers and getting heavy into the survival training. You can still be a prepper and maintain your normal lifestyle. Go to the movies, go out to dinner with friends and do what you normally would. You don't have to become reclusive, grow your hair out and wear camo. There are plenty of average Joes out there who are quietly preparing to survive whatever may come their way.

Now that you know why it is so important to be a prepper, it is time to learn what you need to do to start planning for an uncertain future. The next chapters will take you through each facet of prepping step by step. It is up to you to decide how much you will do.

Chapter 2: The Top 3 Areas Where Most People Lack Preparedness

When it comes to being prepared for a SHTF type of situation, people will fall into one of three categories.

The first group doesn't prepare at all. They live with the belief that they'll somehow be able to handle whatever happens when it happens – or that it won't happen to them at all.

They believe that there will always be adequate food and water supply to take care of their needs and the needs of their loved ones. They think that there will always be shelter for them.

They trust that in the event of a major disaster, the people in government positions where they live will have a plan to make sure everything gets back and up running quickly.

The people who do this are gambling with their lives that everything will turn out okay for them. When a major disaster hits, these are the ones who are scrambling for food and water.

They're trying to hunt down medications, desperate to get what they need to ensure the health and survivability of their family. Because they don't prepare at all, they face huge risks and will literally enter into a fight for survival because they weren't prepared.

The second group of people do prepare somewhat. They realize how important it is that they should be ready to take action or do whatever is necessary to make sure that they and their loved ones are okay.

While they're not completely prepared, they prepare enough to get by for a short term. They'll set aside a week or so of food and water. But they don't have any plans for long-term situations.

They don't prepare for the event that something will disrupt their way of living for months or even years on end. They also don't prepare for the possibilities of having to leave their home and seek a safer location. These people won't find themselves immediately scrambling for necessities, but they will reach that point very quickly indeed.

The third group of people prepares to a much higher level, taking into account all the 'what ifs' and planning as completely as possible. If the world around them collapses into chaos, they're going to survive. They have the food that they need to make sure that they eat for months - and even years.

They have things set aside to generate future food growth. This group makes sure that they have a good supply of water set aside. The means to clean and get to a supply of water when what they have set aside runs out is also part of their plan.

All of the medications needed for each family member are ready to go in the event of a SHTF emergency. They know who's supposed to do what and how they'll react if their plan has to kick into gear.

While they might end up in the middle of a stressful SHTF situation, it won't be a chaotic mess for them when it comes to being able to survive. There are certain supplies and some actions that you need to take that are necessary for your survival and wellbeing.

If you don't make sure these steps are covered, when a SHTF situation does occur, you will lack the ability to have your basic short term as well as long term needs met.

But of all the steps that you need to take, there are three that you need to pay the most attention to – food, water and shelter. Unfortunately, it's these three areas that most people don't prepare well enough or don't prepare at all – because they're so used to never being without them that they take their access to them for granted.

The Importance of a BOB

Everyone should start by having a BOB on hand. This stands for a **Bug Out Bag**. It means that you'll have the supplies together in a bag that will enable you to at least survive for 72 hours.

The purpose of having this bag is so that you can get to it quickly and go. You should never wait until the last minute to pack a bug out bag. You never know if, by putting off gathering the supplies until the last minute, you might put your family in harm's way.

Here's an example of what can happen if you don't have a bug out bag. A SHTF situation occurs and you have to get out fast. You have to leave your home in order to ensure your safety and that of your family.

You round everyone up and you jump in the car. You get going down the road only to find that the road is blocked. There's debris everywhere. You can't get out.

Or, the area has erupted into chaos, people are panicking and it's not even safe to try to get out of your neighbourhood. But it's not safe to stay, either. It's a catch 22, you're stuck.

You might think that not being prepared with a BOB isn't that big of a deal. After all, you have great neighbours and you all help each other out whenever it's necessary.

Borrowing a tool from a helpful neighbour is a far cry from needing help to survive. If it comes down to saving their family or yours, which one do you think they'll pick?

I firmly belief that most people are good people and will help out in an emergency situation, but only to a point. I also believe that these people will band together and try to help out collectively, again only to a point. But in a real SHTF scenario people's priorities change, they will put their loved ones and family before others, and effectively take on a, 'look after number one' attitude, be it unconsciously, but that's what happens. Without realising it, as the situation worsens, protecting your loved ones and family becomes the top priority.

We hear this type of attitude even before any dangerous situations occur – "I'll do anything to protect my family" and even "I'd kill for my family" is something many people say. If that is a mindset now, in times of comfort and easy living, imagine how that is going to escalate in a SHTF situation!

It's not up to someone else to make sure you survive. Or that your family survives. **It's up to you**. When you're forced to flee an area, it might come down to the fact that you have to flee too quickly to take the time to pack up even the basic supplies.

So when you rush out the door, sometimes on foot, you have the clothes on your back. And if you're lucky, you and everyone else are wearing a pair of shoes that they'll be able to walk for miles in!

The minute you're in a SHTF situation, and you understand very clearly how serious it is. Is the minute you need to start putting your prepping plans into action. Without a plan of action everything from now on in will be spur of the moment decisions, and without a real knowledge of what your about to face, your decisions may very well be bad ones.

So you're in a full on panic mode and have rushed out of the door:

The first thing you might notice is that with having to rush from an area, you're in need of water.

Only you don't have any so you have to try to find some. You find some, but it doesn't look clear enough to signal that it's safe to drink. And even if it does look clear, that doesn't mean that it's safe.

Bacteria can lurk in water that you won't be able to see. With no water with you, you're forced to make a choice. Take your chances and drink the water or take your chances and keep moving, hoping you'll find a viable supply down the road somewhere.

If you have small children with you, the need to find water becomes even more urgent. Kids can't withstand the lack of basic necessities as long as an adult can. Their bodies aren't made to handle the same rigors and stresses an adult can. Small children will become a hindrance to your speedy escape plan very quickly.

And if you have a baby who's on formula milk, and there you are without a BOB, which means you don't have formula and you don't have water to give a baby, you are now entering into the realms of serious problems and your SHTF situation is about to get a whole lot worse.

Five minutes into you escape and now you need water - you are in trouble already.

Without a BOB, you don't have any food. When your stomach starts to growl later that day or the next, you might be able to ignore it and push on, trying to find some food.

But food is your body's fuel, so after a while, you're not going to have the energy to keep moving forward. If your family is with you, it will now mean your children are looking to you for food.

The agony and desperation that you'll face if you're responsible for the survival of a child and yet you don't have a way to get that for him will be overwhelming. You're trying to get away from the SHTF situation and you've walked for miles without any luck.

Now that the day is drawing to a close, you have to find shelter - only you're not familiar with living outdoors - especially without supplies. If only you had prepared. By having a BOB would ensure that you'd have shelter when you need it most.

Without it, you're exposed to the elements and so is your family. You'll have an up close and personal experience with rain, with crawling and flying pests, and with cold or hot temperatures.

If you have children, you'll try to huddle together to keep out of the cold or try to make sure they don't come in contact with something while sleeping on the ground that could harm their skin.

While you're on the way, trying to find a way just to survive for a few days so you can wrap your mind around what's going on, you get hurt. Or someone in your family does.

You don't know if you can safely wrap a leaf around a bleeding wound, but you have to because you don't have a first aid kit. If you sprain an ankle or sustain a leg injury, you'll be forced to try to keep on going despite the pain and misery.

If it's a child that can't walk, then you'll have to carry him on your back. Suddenly, you have that added weight in addition to the weight of the world on your shoulders.

When you're forced to bug out, you'll be faced with experiences that you may not have had before in your life. It will come down to a matter of survival and how you respond will determine if you and your family will survive.

You can't live long without water, food and shelter. Those are the three basic needs that you have to cover to make sure that you and those you love are going to be okay.

Now all of the above is a bit extreme, but very possible. If you are escaping from a town or city, you may well be one among a crowd of people doing the same, and all looking for the same basic supplies along the route – quite who gets them is going to make things very uncertain.

In a confirmed SHTF situation you may well all be herded along by government officials or the military towards a holding or evacuation centre.

My view on this: Run in the opposite direction, and fast…. The last words I want to hear are, "I'm from the government and I'm here to help". You will lose all control over what you do, say, eat and sleep. It will be enforced imprisonment to control the people by the so called powers that be. If you have prepared and have a plan, then you will be in complete control of yourself, answerable to no one and probably still very much alive and staying like that.

However, when you don't have a BOB, you won't have the basic tools of survival. You'll have no way to start a fire to boil and sanitize water or cook food, or to defend yourself or your family. You won't have the means to survive what should be an otherwise survivable situation.

When you fail to plan, you plan to fail - as the saying goes. With some things, the price that you'll pay for not planning can fall under an inconvenience or a difficult lesson learned.

But a SHTF situation is a test of survival that, unless you've studied for it, and unless you've prepared for it, won't give you a chance to make up that test. It's not a lesson you learn and fix next time because there may not be a next time for you.

Why You Need a Meet-Up Plan

When a situation arises that calls for you to bug out, you need to have a meet up plan. In situations that call for you to get out, it's usually because something extreme or even life threatening is going on.

When you don't have a plan, it's an open invitation for chaos. And whenever chaos hits, it can cause you to panic. One of the things that happens when people panic is that they make mistakes or bad decisions.

As the survival saying goes:

You can survive 3 seconds if you make a bad decision. 3 minutes without air, 3 days without water and 3 weeks without food.

With heightened emotions, valuable time is often lost trying to figure out what to do. The time to know where you're going to meet is before you ever need to. When a SHTF situation occurs, 'time' will never take your feelings or your family into consideration.

This means that when it occurs, you might be in one area while your significant other would be in another. If you have children, some of them could be at school while another might be at day-care.

Without a plan, you'll waste valuable time - time that could make a difference between safety instead of trying to figure out the best way to bring your family back together again.

Without a plan, you might rush out the door to pick up one child while thinking that your significant other will take care of picking up the other one. If you don't have the ability to communicate with each other because all the phone services are jammed or completely unavailable, you won't know if you should run to keep finding your family members or not.

When you don't have a plan, it will be easy to lose track of family members. If you have elderly parents that you look out for, this can compound a SHTF situation because you'll need to make sure that you or someone else gets to them.

You won't know where to go once you do gather your family if you don't have a meet up plan. But if you do have a meet up plan, you'll know ahead of time the part that everyone is supposed to play in the event of a SHTF disaster, and everyone else knows their role and what to do.

Instead of wasting valuable time trying to figure out what step to take next, you'll be able to focus on what you should be doing - which is getting to safety. Once you have a meet up plan, you'll know the roads you're supposed to take to get there and the area where everyone is supposed to reconnect.

Always plan for zero communication in any SHTF situation as it is very likely to be the case, even if the phone lines are still active they will be overloaded.

Don't forget to have a back-up plan, too – because what if the place you plan to meet at is dangerous now? While a SHTF situation can be extremely stressful, you can lessen the stress of it if you're prepared.

When you know who is going to handle getting your family members and the place where you're all to meet up to be accounted for, it can make everything run smoother.

It will make a bad situation not seem so awful when you have those you love safe and accounted for. The emotional impact will be lessened and you'll be able to concentrate on survival, together.

Even in everyday life the **power of a plan** can make the difference between life and death. Knowing escape routes and fire exits, as well as the quickest routes out of a building is a BASIC prepping skill. In fact, it's not even a skill, it's a necessary piece of ordinary observation meaning you don't have to panic and waste time in an emergency.

It's a scientifically proven fact that people will walk past a fire exit to get to the main entrance door they came in through – even in a fire with alarm bells ringing all around them! Studies have been performed on exactly that scenario.

Once you have established there is an emergency, all 'normal' rules and regulation can be ignored. If there's a door with a big fat private, staff only, do not enter, sign on it, you CAN go through it. In other words in an emergency situation normal rules do not apply.

Having a plan in place before any event will take that disaster from an 'Oh shit **what do I do**' to an 'Oh shit, it's an emergency, **this is what I do**' scenario.

Recognising the level of an emergency dictates your level of planned response – don't leave home without one..!

Chapter 3: Identify The Biggest Risks

One of the first steps in emergency preparedness is identifying your biggest risks. This is largely dependent on your location. You are likely already familiar with the natural disasters most common or expected in your area. If you are a long-time resident, you already know how to react during these situations, but many events can happen almost anywhere and at any time. The most common natural disasters and a few basic tips for preparing:

· Drought – conserve water, plant native or drought-tolerate plants, check for and repair plumbing leaks, reuse water when possible (a bucket placed in the shower can catch water for watering plants or washing clothing)

· Earthquakes – heavy fixtures and furniture should be fastened to walls, breakable should be stored in cabinets rather than on open shelves, plumbing, wiring, gas lines and foundations should be checked for damage on a regular basis, designate safe spots in your home or office to go during an earthquake (under heavy furniture along inside walls)

· Extreme Heat – go to the lowest level of your home, stay indoors and away from the sun, drink plenty of water, check on the elderly, children and pets often

· Floods – move items to upper floors, shut off utilities, stay away from flooded areas and moving water (this includes driving)

· Hurricanes – know your surroundings and plan an evacuation route, reinforce windows and doors when a storm threatens, if in a high-rise stay below the 10th floor

· Landslides – avoid low-lying areas during times of extreme rain or moisture, stay away from steep slopes

· Space Weather – plasma bursts from the sun can disrupt the electrical grid and satellites, plan ahead for power and public utilities outages

· Tornadoes – go to the lowest interior level of your home, stay away from windows, if you are in a vehicle or mobile home try to make it to the closest shelter if time allows

· Tsunamis – move to higher inland ground, stay away from beaches and waterways

· Volcanoes – avoid low-lying areas, beware of mudflows, follow the instructions of local emergency personnel

· Wildfires – shut off fuel supplies, evacuate to a safe location

· Winter Storms – stay indoors, plan ahead for power outages and possible loss of electric heat sources, conserve heating fuel and bundle up

What you may not have fully analyzed are your greatest accidental or man-made disaster possibilities. Do you live near a nuclear power plant? Train tracks (possible chemical spills)? A few potential hazards and preparation tips:

· Nuclear Power Plant Accidents – stay indoors or evacuate to limit radiation exposure, go to the basement or underground, turn off ventilation systems or air conditioning, keep windows and doors closed

· Blackouts – limit the opening and closing of refrigerator and freezer doors in order to maintain safe temperatures as long as possible, if your location is experiencing temperature extremes relocate to a emergency shelter if possible

· Chemical Spills and Hazardous Material Accidents – evacuate immediately when advised, move upstream, uphill or upwind, bring pets indoors and close your home up as much as possible. This includes shutting down ventilation or air conditioning systems. Avoid contact with exposed individuals.

The purpose of the above is to help you identify those hazards you may have overlooked and give you a basic understanding of how to react in that situation. The rest of this book will help you start accumulating the supplies necessary to help you and your family weather a disaster situation in your home without outside assistance. Luckily, preparations for many emergency situations overlap. You do not need separate supplies for numerous individual situations. As an example, with the exception of cold weather gear, our preps for a tornado could also be used during a blizzard.

Bug Out Bag

There is so much buzz about the bug-out bag these days. We will address it first, but please remember this is not the be all and end all of your prepping. This is simply a slimmed down, portable version of your larger stockpile. You are striving to pack enough supplies to last you 3 days, hopefully until help arrives or you reach a more permanent, previously established destination.

The first thing you need when compiling your bug-out supplies is a good bag. Ideally, you are looking for a metal-frame, waterproof hiking bag. This will evenly distribute the weight of your bag's contents, making it easier and less tiring to carry.

Contents of your bug-out bag should include hiking boots and socks, a waterproof windbreaker, high calorie, shelf stable foods like jerky, trail mix, dried fruits and vegetables, first aid supplies, map, compass, water bottle with filter, money, medical and personal contact information, and medications. Pack pre-made meals, which require only hot water. These are readily available in camping and hunting stores or through Amazon. Simply do a search for freeze-dried food pouches. Tea bags, instant coffee and hot cocoa packets are also great for bug-out bags. If the temperatures are cold, these are a quick and easy way to warm up.

Clothing – Outside of your hiking boots and thick socks, your environment will dictate the clothing you should pack. If you live in a colder climate, pack gloves and hats. If you live in a warmer location, you may be able to get by with just a light jacket in the evenings. Everyone should have a hat and sunglasses. A sturdy belt also comes in handy as tools, water bottles, and additional supplies can be tied on to it.

Cleanliness – Hand sanitizer, baby wipes, and soaps are all readily available in travel sizes. Make sure everyone has a clean-up kit in their bag.

Matches, a flashlight, thermal blanket, duct tape, trash bags, a multi-purpose tool, a hand-held radio, and a pocket stove are also great additions to your bags. As these are items that will be shared by your family, distribute them to those who have room in their bags or can carry the additional weight.

Every member of the family needs their own bug-out bag and it should not be so heavy you can't lift it. Regular backpacks are perfect for children's supplies and should include comfort items. Disaster situations are especially frightening for children. Pack travel games or an age appropriate book. There are specially designed pet packs, which will allow your dog to carry his own food and water.

Bug-Out Bags are also perfect for keeping in the car. Just be cognizant of temperature extremes.

Chapter 4: Why Should I Prep?

Prepping can seem like a weird substitute for real hobbies and lots of preppers are portrayed as street corner doomsday prophets just waiting for any sign of chaos to justify their behavior, but when you strip away the disaster-movie gloss and actually look at the reasons for prepping, you will find that it makes a lot of sense and doesn't come with a crazy card.

There are many reasons to start preparing for a partial or full collapse of society, but they all generally fit into three categories:

Natural disaster

Economic depression

Terrorist attack/war

There is nothing quite as unpredictable as the weather, and with climate change brewing more and more aggressive storms, droughts, and erratic temperatures, it is becoming increasingly likely that society as we know it will end because of a major weather event. We have seen it happen in more localized forms, like with hurricanes Katrina and Sandy, earthquakes in Haiti and Chili, and tsunamis in Southeast Asia. Weather events like these shut down the power grid so people are without electricity or water, and the destruction of property creates hundreds of homeless people with no stores to go buy supplies at.

Another reason society could change drastically is the event of a major economic depression. The international market shifts and a country becomes unable to keep up. Currency loses its value and people are forced to turn to stealing or bartering to survive. This is a scenario that has already occurred in most countries, even countries like the United States and in Europe that are so proud of their status and whose people are conditioned to believe societal collapse is impossible. How quickly we forget the poverty and desperation of the Russian Revolution, the Weimar Republic, and the Great Depression. The world has been in a state of perpetual economic collapse for at least ten years now, so who knows when any of those countries could reach the breaking point and dip into complete economic disarray.

War has a reputation for helping the economy, but only if you are on the winning side, and the accumulation of debt and raised taxes to pay for war takes a negative toll on any nation. Terrorist attacks could also lead to societal chaos as the attack could target the food and water supply. It is certainly true at least in America, that if a terrorist attack hit the trucking system, it would only be a matter of weeks before there would be no water, food, fuel, or supplies of any kind and people would be completely on their own to forage for resources. Violence would inevitably break out, as it would in the above scenarios as well. To ensure that you and your family are not victims of this violence, but instead are able to stay safe and distanced from the need to steal and kill to survive, you can start prepping now.

Chapter 5: The Mentality Of Prepping And Survival

We're going to start with the mentality of prepping and survival. Most experts agree that it is the first step in beginning the challenge of survival. This holds true for everything from preparing for the end of the world to finding yourself lost in the mountains to getting stranded on a desert island. The mentality you need for all three of these scenarios and more is fundamentally the same.

Deciding to Survive. This is the first step in putting together a positive mental attitude for prepping. You have a lower chance of surviving if you don't choose to survive first. Deciding to survive may sound easy, but it's actually a challenge on its own. This is because that as soon as you are threatened with something in a remote location, you will automatically react with stress. When you realize you're stranded in the woods or when the grid goes down and you see that you're cut off from the rest of the world it can be overwhelming. The best way to overcome this is to be stubborn and repeatedly tell yourself, "I'm going to survive, I'm going to survive, I'm going to survive. Survive, survive, survive."

Managing Your Stress. Once you have told yourself that you will survive, you can begin to manage the stress you feel. Managing your stress will require equal physical and mental exercise. Physically, take deep and slow breaths, with three seconds in between each breath. This will calm your heart rate down. Mentally, keep reminding yourself that you will survive. Tell yourself that you are a survivor.

Forming a Realistic Strategy. You won't be able to eliminate all of your stress, but if you keep your breathing controlled and tell yourself that you are a survivor, you can manage your stress as much as possible and clear your mind for developing a strategy.

There are a thousand or more different disaster scenarios that could occur, so you'll need to assess your particular situation. This means to take note of your physical and emotional state, your environment, the resources you have available, and the state of the other members in your family and/or group. This means assess how much food, water, ammunition, medical supplies and gasoline you have, what the environment looks like in terms of the weather, the climate, and other people, and if anyone in your group has physical or mental injuries.

Everybody in your group or family who is physically and mentally capable needs a specific task to perform, and someone needs to become the clear leader to set the goals and assign roles. Your first goal is to fully assess the situation and identify the problem. Your second goal to organize the tasks you need to accomplish and how you can accomplish them. Your third goal is to ensure that you can complete these tasks with the resources available to you.

Keeping Morale High. Keeping morale high is essential. It can be tough considering how a disaster situation is life threatening and you'll likely feel anxious, afraid, frustrated and even angry. The best ways to keep up morale is to:

1. Have hope that things will return to normal in the future.

2. Concentrate on the good things that you have accomplished. For example, if you set a task to assess how much food you have, that's an accomplishment no matter how small it is! Dwell on it as you move to the next task, which may be to divide the food for a one week period. Once you have successfully completed this task, dwell on it as well to move onto the next one. You'll see a snowball effect occurring as you repeatedly dwell on the

positive aspects of your situation, and this will give you more creativity to overcome more challenges that will present themselves.

Chapter 6: Potential Causes Of Disaster

It's easy to feel safe in modern society and think that nothing will go wrong. Since you're new to Prepping, I wanted to kick things off by going over some of the things that could cause the potential end of the world as we know it. With the amount of things that could go wrong, it's a wonder that not everyone is preparing for them to be honest.

The Obvious Dangers

Now there are the obvious things that you may want to prepare for such as common natural disasters, but there are far worse and more threatening things out there. That's what I'm going to discuss in this chapter. This isn't just a chapter about weird conspiracy theories that will probably never happen. This stuff is actually possible.

Pandemics

Pandemics are a real cause for concern and something that we have been hearing a lot about over the past few years. New and deadly diseases are appearing faster than ever before. Some believe most of them to be man-made, but wherever they come from, they pose a real threat. Many of the most contagious new diseases have also been weaponized, so if a war breaks out they may be even be purposely released into the population.

Super Volcanoes

We all know what a volcano does when it erupts, we're talking massive damage to the surrounding area. Super volcanoes however are about a million times more powerful. If one of these things were to go off, it would definitely be the end of civilization as we know it. There are 6 super volcanoes on earth so let's hope one doesn't decide to go off any time soon and if it does, well at least will be prepared as best we can!

Solar Flares and Global Warming

Solar flares or solar storms are another big concern. This is basically the sun spewing out a huge electromagnetic pulse or EMP. There is practically no warning as these things will reach us in minutes. They have hit earth before and caused whole telephone wire systems to burst into flames. If one were to hit today in the right spot it would have the potential to knock out the entire electrical grid of any country with ease. Not only this, but Nuclear weapons have a very similar effect and also give off massive EMPs. I have actually written a whole book dedicated to this topic as it's pretty darn interesting (US link – UK link).

Global warming is another huge threat to our way of life and the very existence of humanity. Most people think this is due to fossil fuels and emissions, and that turning off lights or getting an electric car is the answer. In fact it's mainly due to modern animal agriculture and the meat industry so you're much better off going vegetarian if you want to help stop global warming!

Global warming and climate change pose threats in a number of ways. Firstly, as you have probably heard, bees have been dying by the millions since 2006 and they are decreasing in number every year. This causes serious issues with the pollination of crops all over the world. There are about 30,000 other species of living creature going extinct every year, which is faster than at any other point in recorded history. This is causing huge changes to ecosystems and could have potentially catastrophic implications.

Gas Deposits

Some scientists believe that there are massive subterranean methane gas deposits that are in danger of melting due to climate change. If this is true then when they are released into the atmosphere global warming would be increased at a massive rate causing us even more problems.

War

War, or more specifically nuclear war, is also a distinct possibility. The most likely countries to launch nuclear weapons at each other are the United States and Russia but this would have massive implications for people the world over.

Financial Collapse

There is also financial breakdowns that could cause the structure of society to fall flat on its face in a matter of hours. If a complete financial breakdown were to occur and currency was made useless, chaos would descend on the population immediately with everyone looting and taking whatever they could find.

There are other risks such as asteroids and massive tsunamis, the Oxford University even released a study that listed artificial intelligence as the most likely cause for the apocalypse at 10% probability. However I think what I have mentioned in this chapter are the main concerns for most people. So hopefully now you have a better idea of why people do get prepared for one of these eventualities to happen. Now let's talk about exactly how to prepare.

Chapter 7: What Is Shtf Prepping

Creating an SHTF Survival Disaster Preparedness Plan

Planning your long term arrangements and technique, in case of a disaster, is a standout amongst the most basic parts of effectively surviving long term. In the event that you don't have an arrangement set up, or your arrangement is fragmented and missing essential components, you won't recover from it. In this segment, I'll discuss probably the most vital inquiries you'll have to ask yourself and have replied before beginning.

* Where will you take a sanctuary after the catastrophe?

* Do you have a reinforcement shield arrange for when something happens to your fundamental safe house?

* Is your shelter near a true blue water source that you can without much of a stretch get to?

* Is your shelter warm, dry, and ready to be secured from assailants?

* Do you have admittance to both sustenance and shelter in a similar area, or are they isolate from each other.

* What number individuals will you have in your gathering?

* Do you have an arrangement set up to keep your sustenance secure and dry?

* Will you have distinctive stockpiles in numerous areas?

* How long can your stockpiles last?

* What is your arrangement for renewing your stockpile, and whatever other apparatuses, or weapons you have to survive long haul?

* Do you have an exhaustive emergency treatment unit?

* How will you guard your family or gathering from an assailant?

* Do you have any weapons preparing or restorative preparing? If not, do you anticipate getting any?

As you may have seen there are a considerable measure of things you'll have to consider before making a SHTF catastrophe readiness survival arrange. Simply after you've worked out the responses to these vital inquiries would you be able to truly start to get an arrangement set up.

I get a kick out of the chance to think about my arrangement being separated into three distinctive principle stages. The clench hand stage is my transient arrangements (months 1-4). The second stage is my mid-term arranges (5 months – 1 year). The last stage is my long haul arrange (1 year +). Each of these stages ought to be completely thoroughly considered and arranged for.

In the event that you neglect to do this, you could wind up prepping inaccurately, or wind up squandering prepares you invested energy in, because of lack of foresight. Stockpiled, your proportions are the most straightforward part of the procedure. The harder parts include knowing to what extent your prepping will last, how will utilize them, and what you're arrangements are the point at which you're stockpile runs low.

I recommend keeping point by point records of the greater part of your prepare and each thing in your stockpile. It's essential to know the amount of everything when you added the thing to your stockpile, the close date of your sustenance, any guidelines required on the most proficient method to work something you've bought, and a timetable for turning your nourishment so you're continually eating things before they ruin and go to squander.

The better you keep these records and the additional time you spend arranging your stockpile, the better your odds of surviving long haul. This may all vibe somewhat overwhelming at to start with, however I guarantee you these are fairly basic propensities to frame once you go ahead. The sooner you show signs of improvement. Inside no time, these propensities will turn out to be second nature and a piece of your day by day schedule.

Kindly don't keep your preparing records on the web. At the point when a crisis happens, you'll likely lose the Internet and potentially your energy on the off chance that you don't have some sort of generator. On the off chance that you don't have an approach to get to every one of your records, then your work arranging and classifying everything will have been done futile. In a crisis circumstance, learning is an intense favorable position.

The more you have the happier you'll be. I recommend once you've mapped out your arrangement; you then think of an optional one on the off chance that the main arrangement is included. You'll need to have escape courses and interchange areas chose ahead of time in the event that something drives you from your base of operations. I would have some bug out areas scouted, and I would conceal a few supplies along your escape courses that you can reach if necessary. Having possibilities is a critical part of any fiasco readiness arrange. Things infrequently work out precisely as we imagine they will. Giving yourself different alternatives will just enhance your odds. Actually, I have numerous techniques and arrangements mapped out for every sort of real calamity. Along these lines I have an arrangement that is particularly customized to whatever kind of SHTF circumstance my family and I discover us in. I likewise keep stockpiles in a three other bug out areas, ought to specific ranges get to be distinctly perilous and hazardous.

At last, and the significance of this can't be focused on enough CONSTANTLY BE DRILLING! You can make arrangements till your face turns blue, however in the event that you can't execute those arrangements appropriately, and afterward you were simply squandering your time.

When I started running drills, I was stunned at the measure of things we missed in the arranging stages. That, as well as we experienced difficulty executing our arrangements accurately in an opportune manner. Keep in mind, in crisis circumstance things may be more troublesome as you'll need to manage larger amounts of stress and dread. It required some investment yet now when my family drills we're a very much oiled unit.

Since I live basically out and about with my family RVing around the nation we have to penetrate all the more frequently, in light of the fact that there's significantly more factors included relying upon our area at the time. Keep in mind, when a calamity happens you have to know you're any arrangements all around. You need to have the capacity to respond off of impulse, and don't have thought too long on what you're next strides will be. I propose penetrating in any event once per month, at various circumstances of the day, and dependably concentrate on tweaking or enhancing any regions you think require it.

The Preppers Checklist

1. Make a fastener for all your imperative papers and records. This is a critical asset to have helpful. It's great for huge crises as well as littler crises that may come up in your regular day to day existences. A portion of the things you ought to incorporate into your cover are birth certificates, social security cards, divorce & marriage documents, passports, insurance

and mortgage papers, medical records, diplomas, prescription lists and immunization records. You'll need to keep this fastener some place safe yet open. I have my cover put away securely in a little flame resistant box situated in a simple to achieve shrouded safe.

2. Make a rundown of aptitudes you'll need to begin learning. At that point assume your rundown and position every one of the aptitudes in the request of most significance to slightest significance. That way, you can start adapting new abilities in view of their need level. A few abilities to consider adding to your rundown incorporate self-protection, weapons preparing, medical aid, cooking, planting, and chasing.

3. Make a nourishment and supplies diary. Utilize these diaries to archive all that you and your family expend throughout one week. This ought to be a greatly careful bookkeeping, so kindly don't skirt things or forget stuff since you don't believe it's

sufficiently critical for consideration. Having a precise evaluation will go far in giving you a thought on the best way to make the perfect rundown for your long haul supplies and sustenance stockpiling.

4. Make a point by point survival arrange and a security anticipate how you'll protect your property from conceivable interruption. You'll need to comprehend what measures you'll have set up to prevent assailants and what weapons, ammo and rigging you'll require so as to appropriately safeguard your property. You ought to likewise have escape courses arranged and substitute areas to fall back to on the off chance that required.

5. Do a full examination of every one of your vehicles and a through and through assessment of your home. You have to go over every last bit of both your vehicles and home to discover and settle any issues you run over. You need to start getting every one of the issues settled now before catastrophe strikes and make settling

things a great deal more troublesome. You likewise need to ensure your vehicles are fit as a fiddle, on the off chance that you ever need to bug out of your living arrangement rapidly. The exact opposite thing you need is a breakdown amid a crisis circumstance.

6. Contingent upon your living circumstance and space you're working with, I would recommend you start cutting and putting away kindling. Having enough wood to use as fuel will be critical in a SHTF circumstance. This is particularly valid if a catastrophe happens amid the colder winter months when the requirement for extra warmth is at a premium.

7. Get ready bug out packs for both you and any relatives. Everybody ought to have their own sack, and know precisely what's inside them. These packs should be prepared ahead of time, so in case you're compelled to leave immediately despite everything you'll be readied.

8. Start a wellness schedule. Off lattice living requires a great deal of diligent work and assurance. The better shape you're in physically the better you'll have the capacity to meet the new requests you'll be compelled to manage to survive. I appreciate climbing and climbing. It helps me remain fit as well as taking in a variety of aptitudes by being out in nature in the meantime.

9. Start your stockpile. Other than nourishment, you have to stock up on fuel, family supplies, devices, weapons, batteries and an assortment of different things I'll address later in this book. I recommend you additionally stock up on things to keep you and your family engaged amid down time. This incorporates things like recreations and books. I'd additionally prescribe beginning an accumulation of DIY, how to, restorative, and cookbooks. In the event that something turns out badly once SHTF, you won't have the capacity to call

another person for offer assistance. Rather, it will be dependent upon you to make sense of an answer for the issue. Having these books close by can be a genuine lifeline.

10. Make a dental unit and emergency treatment pack. These ought to be as extensive as you can make them. In the event that things go south, you'll see that getting medication or medicinal administrations will turn out to be amazingly troublesome if not unthinkable. I likewise propose getting some fundamental restorative preparing on the most proficient method to treat minor wounds, wounds and smolders. I would likewise take a course in CPR preparing.

Chapter 8: Why You Need To Prepare

Why should you prepare at all?

The reason most people ask this question is that they have no personal experience of a large scale disruptive event and they believe that should such an event occur, which they think is unlikely, the Government will step in and save them.

Unfortunately they are wrong on both counts as recent history shows us, the aftermath of the effects on New Orleans of hurricane Katrina being a sobering reminder that disasters can strike with devastating consequences with little warning.

Widespread flooding and damage to property displaced the local population and fears and shortages led to widespread unrest resulting in looting on a scale that forced local law enforcement to abandon search and rescue operations to bring it under control.

So far as government intervention is concerned, the civil defense program which was initiated in the 1950s and which was responsible for duck and cover drills in schools, structures being designated as official fallout shelters and the distribution of survival leaflets, was largely abandoned in the 1970s. Only since the September 11th attacks and hurricane Katrina has there been an increase in government interest in preparing for emergencies.

With the current political instability around the world, the threat of terrorist attacks and even war is very real. If that wasn't enough, we have the prospect of global warming which brings with it the threat of rising sea levels and failing crops as well as natural events such as volcanic eruptions, earthquakes and tsunamis to contend with.

It is up to each of use to do what we can to be prepared. Recent events have shown that we cannot rely on others to do it for us. You may find yourself in a situation where you need to react quickly to protect your family, your home, your assets and belongings, even your life.

You can't stop these events from happening and you probably wont come out of them completely unscathed however much you prepare, but if you take action now, it could mean the difference between experiencing a complete disaster and surviving little more than a major inconvenience.

WHAT EVENTS YOU NEED TO BE PREPARED FOR

The number of potential events that could have serious consequences is huge. We live in troubled times and ignore the lengths some people will go to in the name of religious or political beliefs at our peril.

Technological advances of the last few decades have done a lot to make out lives better, but they have also resulted in an exponential growth in man's ability to do harm to man.

Nature is something we can't ignore either. We may not be at any more risk from natural events today than our ancestors were at any time in human history, but we are able to understand better what nature could throw at us and if we prepare for them, we have much more chance of surviving events that in the past have destroyed entire civilizations.

Not all events that you could need to get through are threats to the world or society.

You could have to get by when a local emergency happens, such as a localized flood or a power outage. On the scale of disasters, these rank low, but from a personal point of view, having to defend your home from a rising river, heat a home when there is no power, or try to save food in the freezer from going bad when there is no electricity to keep it running could seem pretty serious at the time.

Moving up the scale, disruptions to the movement of food or supplies due to extensive flooding or a bridge collapse could hit you hard and worse still, an epidemic or the consequences of a terrorist attack which could come in many forms including bombs and biological weapons, would be even more difficult to deal with.

Not all threats are physically destructive. An EMP (electromagnetic pulse) can damage and disrupt electronic equipment which could result in widespread breakdown of communication services and the internet.

We rely on the world's financial systems to supply us with food, water, supplies and information. Any large scale disruption to the power grid or the means of electronic communication would cause a meltdown of the world's financial markets and lead to an unfathomable number of disastrous consequences.

These threats don't have to be man made. A natural disaster of gigantic proportions such as the eruption of a super volcano or a meteor strike could have devastating consequences for our inter-dependent connected world.

At its most extreme, a sufficiently large scale disaster event could cause the collapse of society as we know it and it could happen far more quickly than you can imagine.

THE POTENTIAL CONSEQUENCES OF EVENTS

You may find yourself dealing with one or more of a large number of consequences when a disruptive or threatening event occurs.

A shortage of basic necessities such as food, water, fuel and gasoline could be caused by several different events from a local flood to a terrorist attack or natural event such as an earthquake.

A disruption to the electricity supply caused by a deliberate act or natural causes could result in a loss of communication, no heating and air conditioning, damage to frozen or chilled food, financial disruption, both internet banking due to having no access to the internet, and banks or ATM's being unable to function.

High rainfall could cause localized flooding resulting in disruption to travel both for you and supplies in and out of your neighborhood as well as putting you, your property and your belongings at risk.

A fire in your property or that of a neighbor, or more seriously at a local factory, power plant, refinery or other commercial building storing chemicals or other hazardous materials could cause risk to life or property due to poisonous air, unsafe drinking water or radiation.

In more extreme cases you might find yourself facing chaos, lawlessness or violence if the consequences of the event are so severe that it causes a breakdown in society. Social unrest quickly follows disruptive events, triggering looting and riots as people do what they are driven to do to survive and protect their loved ones.

The response of the authorities to such a threat to local or national society would be the implementation of martial law resulting in restrictions on travel and curfews.

Where you live and your own personal circumstances have a bearing on how many of the consequences described above could be an issue for you and how serious a threat they would be, but hopefully I have given you some things to think about. Even doing as little as storing extra food and water against a local emergency could make a big difference to you and your family if you find yourself having to deal with any one of these situations.

WHAT YOU WILL NEED TO DO TO SURVIVE

There are two expressions of nautical origin that we all use regularly; batten down the hatches and weathering the storm.

These days we use those expressions to cover getting through all kinds of unforeseen and unplanned-for situations. In the case of less serious disruptive events that is exactly what you need to do, wait them out until they are over.

For more serious events you may need to evacuate your home to avoid the risk of personal injury or death, retreat to a place of safety or find shelter if the situation results in your being out of doors overnight or for a longer duration.

You may need to protect your family and loved ones which may involve you traveling to collect them if they are away from home.

You may have to deal with natural and man made threats including fires, floods and other natural disasters, organized attacks, accidental explosions, violence and looting caused by civil unrest.

You may need to give first aid or more serious medical treatment to people who have been injured, or treat yourself if you have no access to medical care due to being cut off away from society.

If the situation persists for a prolonged period and you are out of reach of immediate help, you may need to find food, fresh water and fuel for a fire.

You need to be prepared for any and all of these situations. Even just having a plan and a store of basic necessities will help.

In the next chapter we will look at what you will need to have ready if you are to cope and survive when a disaster strikes.

WHAT YOU WILL NEED IN AN EMERGENCY

There are lots of things you need to have ready when the time comes to react to a disruptive or threatening event. Some of these are quite simple and can be picked up at the local store such as canned food, others take time to prepare such as an evacuation plan or safe location if you need to evacuate.

This chapter is written as an overview list so you can use it as a checklist to plan your own preparations. In the next chapter we will look in more detail at what you need how you get them together. Some things are basic and will be needed whatever the situation, some will only be relevant if you are staying where you are, others will be needed if you have to evacuate for a long or short period.

You may need to put together different plans and resources to cope with a variety of situations you may encounter, so use the lists in this chapter for outline planning and refer to the next chapter to fill out those plans in detail.

Basic Essentials

Food

Water

Toiletries and hygiene supplies

Cleaning supplies

First aid and medical supplies

Clothing

Household items

Basic tools and survival equipment

Water purification

Cooking equipment and fuel

Lighting

Gardening equipment and seeds

Fishing gear

Weapons and hunting gear

Energy sources

Maps and Guides

Map of local area

Edible plant guide

Outdoor cooking guide

First aid manual

Natural remedies guide

Means of escape/evacuation

Transportation

Gasoline/fuel

Means of providing shelter

Safe location

Camping equipment

Means of contact/communication

Cellphones

Two way radio

Whistle

Flares

Mirror

Agreed meeting place

Emergency plans

For when you are staying put (lockdown)

For when you have to evacuate

ID and other documentation

Photo id/passport

Birth certificate

Social security card

Medical records

Banking and insurance documents

Contact information

Money and Barter items

Cash

Gold and silver jewelry

Luxury goods: candy, coffee, soap, toilet paper etc.

Luxury/Entertainment Items

Cards, games, dice

Musical Instruments

Paper, pens, pencils

Books

Chapter 9: Prepping: Getting Started

When disaster strikes, many of us hope that the government will be there to help. And it does. But one thing is true; even with all the budgetary allocation for disaster preparedness, when disaster strikes, the victims face it first hand and before any help can show up, you will probably have spent several hours, days or even weeks before help can come depending on where you are and the nature of the disaster. Well, unfortunately, that's how life is and in as much as we may want to say that the government might fail in its responsiveness, it may not be practically possible to help everyone when disaster strikes especially when the area affected is pretty large and is densely populated. And even if you were to go to your nearby rescue center, the truth is that they may be pretty ill prepared for an emergency thus making it almost impossible for them to manage the large group of those in need. Soon, you will start fighting for staples when the rescue center cannot keep up with the number. So what should you do at such times? Well, if you were not prepared, the best thing you can hang on is hope. But when you **start prepping**, you have control over what happens during a survival situation. You don't just wait for the government and aid agencies to rescue you. Instead, you take deliberate measures to ensure that you have everything you need to survive. But even with all the prepping, one thing is true; your mindset is your biggest asset when it comes to prepping. With the right mindset, you can do anything and overcome any challenge you may face. But whatever you do, it is important to keep in mind that:

3 minutes without air is enough to leave you unconscious

3 hours without synchronized body temperature is enough to leave you unconscious

3 days without water will leave you dead

3 weeks without food is enough to kill you

This means one thing; as you prepare for survival, you need to make sure that you prep in order i.e. shelter followed by water then finally food. With proper planning, assessment, and re-evaluation, you should be able to avoid/minimize panic and negative mindset and with that, your chances of survival will be drastically increased. So how do you prep? Where do you start? Well, it starts with preparing a survival pantry. Let's learn how to do that in the next chapter.

Setting Up The Pantry

Without food and water, you are pretty much doomed no matter what else you may be having. As such, before you can do anything else, the first thing you need to do is to set up a survival pantry (you can keep this in a survival bag or in a fixed pantry in your house) where you will keep enough food to sustain you for a few days into the disaster. For this, you will need to consider the perceived impact and the period you think the disaster may last. Don't just stockpile stuff that you have never eaten. Instead, stock stuff that you eat daily to avoid instances of discovering that you cannot eat something after wasting all the space and energy to keep a certain food. Nonetheless, what you pack in your pantry (or survival bag) is truly up to you but as you do that, you need to consider a few pointers:

Macronutrients: You should aim to have all the essential macronutrients in your pantry to ensure that you have a balanced meal. This should ideally comprise 5-20% proteins for toddlers & babies, 10-35% proteins for adults, and 10-30% proteins for kids and teens. As for carbs, you should aim for about 45-65% and for fats; you should aim to have 30-40% for babies & toddlers, 25-35% for kids & teens, and 20-35% for adults. As for the calories, you should aim for at least 1200 calories.

Tip about meals: Aim for about 500-700 calories per meal for each of the three meals then calculate that for the number of days that you want the food to last you. To help you stockpile fast, try to buy an extra item every time you go shopping. You will soon find yourself with a good quantity of such items. But don't just keep them forever; try to cycle such items in your everyday consumption to ensure you don't end up with expired food products. You can try to keep the new food at the back and those that have stayed for awhile at the front.

Tip: Keep in mind that there is something referred to as food fatigue caused by taking the same old food every other day. As such, don't just assume that any food is food during a survival situation. Try to have variety if you truly want to have a smooth time. You can pack such things like:

45-60 ready to eat meals packed in vacuum pouch bags.

Salt and pepper to make food tasty

Seeds: these are easy to pack and are light to carry around. Of course, if you are to survive in the wild for longer, you will somehow need to figure out a way of growing your own foods and not just relying on fish and meats. You can pack squash, corn, tomatoes, cantaloupe, lettuce, early carrots, broccoli, watermelon, Swish chard, onions, red beets, pumpkins, potatoes (white), cabbage, spinach, various herbs, sweet potatoes etc.

Grains

These will be made up of energy giving food and they include; pasta, rice, oats, cereals, pancake mixes, stuffing mixes and other similar foods.

Vegetables

These will serve as your major source of vitamins and minerals and they include a variety of canned vegetables.

Fruits

You can get additional fruit supply through foraging, but you need to pick your own fruits just in case. Items in this category will include all canned fruits and fruit juice that come in containers.

Protein

Basic food in this category include; canned salmon, canned tuna, peanut butter, canned lentils, canned legumes, canned soups, eggs and dried legumes.

Diary Food

These are other sources of proteins that will be needed and they will include packed dry milk, cheese, and yoghurt, canned liquid milk, soy milk etc.

Other Items

These are other miscellaneous items you will need in your survival bag and they include wine especially non-alcoholic ones because you will need to stay alert at all times to survive during this period. Others you will need will include: condiments like sauce, olive oil, butter, vinegar, ketchup, salt, ginger, pepper, dried herbs, sugar, and honey.

Tips For Stocking Your Bag

☐Stick To Canned Items

You should always stick to canned items unless you are sure that your stay is a very short one. Canned foods can last for months if not years before they expire. That is the best option for you, not fresh foods that will get spoiled in a matter of days.

☐Dried Items

You should always choose dried food to fresh ones; the moisture in dried foods has been extracted making them to last longer than fresh food.

☐Think Long Term

You have to think long term when packing your pantry bag because you never can tell how long you will stay out there before help comes your way. So you need to include as many items as you can carry to last for a long time.

☐Always Check For Expiration Dates

If you're buying canned food, it is advised that you take time to check the expiration dates for every item before purchase. Try to go for items with longer expiration dates.

☐Balanced Meal

When packing your survival bag, ensure that the food in the bag is able to make you a balanced meal without your secondary source of food. That is why from the list I made on how to pack a pantry bag, I ensured that all the classes of food were present in the list to some extent. You need well balanced meals to stay fit, and fortify your immune system.

Important Note:

Even as you pack various foods, ensure to carry cookware; you can use a backpacker's cooking set, which you can fasten to the outside of the bug out bag or on your belt. But as you do this, ensure to carry one fork, a table knife and a strong spoon. You should also think of having a thick iron skillet or a cooking pot if need be.

Keep in mind that fire is life when it comes to survival. It will keep you warm at night and will help you prepare various foods comfortably. As such, don't under pack when it comes to prepping for fire because without anything else, knowing how to light a fire can keep you alive since you can hunt, catch various insects and prepare various foods. As such, ensure to have such things like 3 steel flint fire starters, bic lighters, waterproof matches and a hand lens.

And even as you do all that, you will also need to set up a survival bag i.e. the bug out bag that you will be carrying around with you or even place one at different places like in your car, your office, your home and other areas just to ensure that you always have enough survival stuff to survive for several days if disaster strikes.

Chapter 10: What You Need

Before you pick a camp and start navigating through the wilderness, it is important to plan the right backpack full of the stuff you will want to survive, but roughing it does not mean struggling. In this chapter, we will assist you in identifying the essential gear, tools, and clothing items that are handy when living outdoors.

1. Survivalist's Tool Kit: Necessities for covering any contingency.

Contingencies in the wilderness abound, so it is essential to plan for as many as possible. A compass will help you in finding your way; even better is a handheld GPS device. Flashlights and glow sticks help you in finding your way in the dark, and a flare gun will help others find you in an emergency. For setting up camp, Paracord or rope, a tarp, duct tape, and cable ties are essential. Also essential is a great multi-tool, folding shovel, and gloves. Include water-proof matches, a lighter, and fire starter kit; redundancy is a good thing in this instance. In a small tin, store fishhooks and line, razor blades, stitching needles and thread, safety pins, nails, a small magnet, and a little cash.

2. How to Pack: Simple hints for packing your backpack.

A well-packed backpack is considered necessary for your comfort and safety. Poor weight distribution results in muscle aches and needless pressure on your backbone. Place heavy gadgets – water, meals, and cooking tools – in the middle of your pack, close to your body. Use medium weight items – clothes, tarps, and rain gear – to cushion the heavier items, securing them so the load does not shift while you are hiking. Store your sleeping bag on the back of your backpack or tie it to the bottom. Purchase items that you are likely to need regularly in the side and outer pockets – compass and map, sunglasses, toilet paper, and trowel, sunscreen, bug repellent, pocketknife, flashlight, snacks, and a small towel.

3. What to Wear: Prepare for layering

Depending upon the geographic area of the wilderness region you are journeying in, and the time of year, temperatures can range dramatically over the duration of 24 hours. Layer your apparel to save heat and keep your weight light. A fleece jacket, windbreaker, and waterproof outer jacket should be sufficient to address worst-case scenarios. A pair of sandals and water shoes round out your wardrobe with gloves, a hat, and a headband.

4. Useful multi-tools: Must-have survival equipment

For flexibility, a terrific multi-tool is a camper's best friend, and there are many types on the market. When comparing the want for best capabilities and the device's weight, it will become apparent that less complicated is better. Search for a multi-tool that has an ordinary and serrated blade, pliers with a twine cutter, carbide knife sharpener, bottle, and can opener, and a lanyard loop. Pay close attention to the materials and quality; look for titanium handles, 154CM metallic blades, and 420 stainless steel construction. If you plan on carrying a small hatchet for cutting firewood, consider a multi-tool hatchet and select that instead.

5. Food: What to pack

Plan a menu of quick and light foods that are easy to prepare. The type and amount of meals you carry will vary, depending on if you are journeying in a vehicle or trekking deep into the wilderness on foot. If you are carrying everything in your backpack, take dry and dehydrated ingredients that you can cook with hot water. A variety of pre-packaged meals are available at most camping stores, or you could make them at home.

6. Prepackaged meals: just add water

Prepackaged meals are the perfect camping food – light-weight, handy, and easy to prepare. Many prepackaged meals are available for purchase, you may buy bulk, choose the varieties of food you want, and have fun by making your own. For lunch, try 1/3 cup of dry couscous, ½ cup freeze-dried vegetables and let's not forget about dessert; how does a blended fruit cobbler sound?

7. Bandanas: many uses for a humble piece of cloth

Bandanas take up very little space, have many uses, and might even be worn as jewelry. As a medical device, use it as a tourniquet, wound dressing, smoke masks, or sling. Protect your head from the sun, make a sweatband, or tie back your hair. If you end up lost or disoriented, a brightly colored bandana makes an easy-to-spot signal; tear strips to mark your trail.

Best Survival Foods to Stockpile

What are the best survival meals to stockpile for an emergency at this level? What do you want to get now before than it is too late and before chaos erupts — and while you still have access to cash.

What makes the best survival foods for an emergency?

A wide variety of catastrophic disasters may occur. It could be a terrorist attack with a WMD or the feared EMP attack that shuts down power throughout a country, interrupting transportation and shipping for many weeks, resulting in massive food shortages.

It is clear in recent years that a huge disaster can strike any time and any place. Whether it is a man-made disaster or an unprecedented natural disaster, you should start preparing by stocking up on the best survival supplies, so you are prepared for anything.

Non-perishable foods make the best survival food

In the heat of the moment, or several weeks in advance, you are going to want foods that help you in meeting dietary needs, that have a high calorie content, and easy meals likely to vanish first from pantries.

There are survival food kits

If you need to get a head-start on building up your stockpile, there are a few outstanding survival meal kits available that will let you do that. No one knows when catastrophe will strike, and you will be kicking yourself if you had plans to build a stockpile but started too late. That's where these food kits come in. Most of them have 25-30 years of shelf-life and include a wide variety of flavors. Granted, with these emergency meals kits, you will be paying more per calorie/per meal than if you build your stockpile. But if you are trying to get a head-start because you know something catastrophic could take place at any time, it is probably a good idea to stock up on a meal kit ASAP so you at least have the beginnings of a long-term stockpile of survival meals.

Weight and Packaging May Be a Factor

Which foods can you get the most of and get the most out of? It is crucial to remember calorie needs, ease of use/preparation, shelf life, and even "weight" factored in. Why is weight a factor? What if you and your family must evacuate an area on foot and have nothing but survival backpacks and or suitcases? You will regret having stocked up on a lot of canned foods when you realize just how much they weigh. The best survival food balances the weight in opposition to nutritional and caloric value. This is something you must pay particular attention to in case you also plan on having survival equipment with you.

Canned food is heavy and not portable – because of this, if push comes to shove, it will be hard to travel with a large quantity of it. Canned food must be a part of your survival diet though — it may be the food that allows you to get through the first few weeks, as long as you do not have to evacuate or travel (especially on foot). When you have canned food, you should have a survival multi-tool with you (instead of a can opener). A can opener is a single-use tool – and generally, you need to avoid those.

With that said, the top recommended survival meals are…

Some Best Survival Foods

1.) Canned Alaskan wild Salmon

Canned Alaskan wild salmon is rich in protein and wholesome fat like omega 3s. Search for "Alaskan wild salmon," and you are likely to find salmon with little to no environmental contaminants, which can sometimes show up in other canned fish from other parts of the world. Salmon may not be your preference now but know the Inuit people (local people of Alaska and northern Canada) on a conventional diet are known for low counts of heart attack and stroke, which is attributed to their long term, non-stop diet of fish.

Like tuna fish, you can eat canned Alaskan wild salmon right out of the can, without cooking — though, if you have leftovers, it is going to have to be refrigerated where it will be good for the next three to four days. If refrigeration is not an option, plan to share the salmon with two to three other people at a time, so nothing is going to waste. Down to its lengthy shelf life and exceptional protein content, and it is on the top of our list when it comes to the best survival foods. It tastes excellent too!

2.) Brown rice

Brown rice is high in calories and protein, in addition to essential vitamins and minerals such as iron. As a dry, non-perishable meal, brown rice has a long shelf-life making it a great survival food. Brown rice has one problem though: generally, it needs to be boiled for several minutes. Sometimes, in a long-term emergency where no electricity is available, the last thing you need to do is use precious gasoline for cooking food for this duration of time; whether or not that's on propane, butane, or wood-burning stove. So, for an extended survival emergency, in which you are stocking up your pantry, "brown rice warm cereal" is likely better because it cooks in just five to eight minutes and remains filled with vitamins and calories (one cup of brown rice warm cereal contains 600 calories, 12 grams of protein, and 16% of the daily recommended amount of iron and is easily rationed out into smaller quantities).

Stock up on brown rice

Prepare proper grain storage: storing brown rice and other grains in a nice, dry area in large plastic containers is essential to preserve freshness. The store-bought varieties of brown rice and brown rice cereal may only have a shelf life of three – six months. So, you will want a plan to rotate your brown rice cereal every three months so that it is eaten in your own home (makes an easy, wholesome breakfast and is an alternative to sugar-packed cereals).

Long-term storage: due to its three-month shelf-life, if you will decide not to rotate your brown rice cereal, a better value for your money's worth of brown rice for long-term storage is to go with a freeze-dried version from Wise Company or Mountain House (with these companies you are not limited to only brown rice).

Techniques to make the best survival foods

With that said, you can use the same techniques to preserve other nonperishable ingredients that large food producers sell such as Wise Company and Mountain House. You can do it affordably (saving yourself a lot of money on long-term survival food), which means that you could find the money to buy extra food in bulk.

You will need special food storage materials (foil pouches and oxygen absorption packets) and five-gallon plastic buckets, which may be used as containers for storing many foil pouches of meals at a time. We go into more detail in our article, "The Best Emergency Meal Methods" – these techniques will help you obtain remarkable shelf-life for a wide variety of foods (such as 10 – 25 years of shelf-life). If you want to be prepared for a real, long-term disaster, it might make sense to research those techniques. A few of the best survival ingredients on this list may be preserved by using the techniques mentioned in the article about emergency food strategies.

3.) Dried beans

Kidney beans, black beans, garbanzo beans, lima beans, pinto beans, and others are all high in calories, have a lot of protein per serving and also contain several essential vitamins and minerals. Dried beans are available in larger quantities than canned beans and they weigh less. The key difference is that you need to add water and let most beans to soak for many hours before eating. Split peas, for instance, have a shorter soak time. Split peas are a part of the dried bean family with some of the same nutrients and minerals. Ultimately, dried beans have long shelf lifestyles. Dried beans will last in the trunk of your car, your office survival kit, and in your pantry of survival meals at your property or cabin.

Stock up on dried beans

Will you need to feed a few other mouths during a disaster? A huge supply of dried beans is significantly cheaper for the amount of people you could feed, can go a long way, and are a great meal to carry in a backpack, compared to canned beans, which you are better off leaving behind.

4.) Bulk nuts

Look for the bulk seed/nut section of your grocery store, and specifically for unsalted and unshelled (if possible). You want to choose survival ingredients with a low salt content. Peanuts, almonds, sunflower seeds, and several other nuts/seeds typically sold in grocery store bulk food section are high in essential vitamins and minerals, essential fatty acids, and have a large amount of protein. They are also quite light-weight.

At the same time, invest money into air-tight food storage bins, including plastic packing containers or glass jars. You can expand shelf life by storing those in the fridge, although most bulk dry foods will keep up to a few months (make sure to check expiration dates), if kept in a nice, dark, area.

5.) Peanut butter

It is filled with protein and essential fatty acids, in addition to includes many essential nutrients and minerals (including copper and iron). For the healthiest option, choose "natural" brands such as Skippy Natural Peanut Butter. Just a couple tablespoons a day of peanut butter can help a person continue to survive during a time of food scarcity (throughout a disaster, one of your strategies to live to tell the tale is to acknowledge that it is time to cut calories — most people consume more calories a day than they need to survive. Cutting calories means your food will last longer, at the same time helping you lose extra weight, making evacuation on foot sooner or later easier than if you are carrying around extra pounds).

6.) Trail mix

A favorite of hikers, trail mix has a variety of components, such as raisins, peanuts, other nuts, and often portions of chocolate. The simple sugars in the raisins, chocolate, and dried fruit may be a quick morale booster and supply of short-term energy. Trail mix is a way to include dried fruit in your survival diet.

7.) Energy bars and chocolate bars

There are energy bars available in every flavor. Look for brands with a high calorie count in addition to lots of protein and a wide range of nutrients.

Chocolate bars – chocolate can be a brief source of energy and an exceptional morale booster, while also being high in calories. (Chocolate is also likely to end up a commodity in demand in the weeks and months following a catastrophe.)

8.) Beef jerky

Look for "natural" brands of beef, turkey, and other meats, which does not contain any or as much of the unhealthy ingredients in other jerky brands. What is jerky? Jerky is a tasty piece of dried meat. Dried meat is a time-tested survival food used by Native Americans and American pioneers alike and as well as by primitive cultures around the world. While primitive methods use smoking and sun drying methods to create "jerky," nowadays, commercial techniques of drying meat do that on a far large scale. You have options: One is to buy the smaller serving packages at the store or to buy your dried meat in bulk and have it shipped to you directly.

9.) Coffee / instant coffee

Even if you do not, a person in your group is likely to consider the coffee (or in reality caffeine) crucial and may be tired, lethargic, and get headaches without it. Coffee does not need to be a top priority, but being able to get it will be something many people in your party are likely to be happy about. It is a short-term mood booster and good for morale. And it is another thing that might be traded like a commodity in a crisis situation.

10.) Sea vegetables / powdered super vegetables

A popular item advertised in health foods stores these days are the sea vegetables that are available in powdered form or tablet. In a time of disaster, most places are going to be short on fresh produce. Sea vegetables are first-rate meals, full of vitamins, nutrients and health benefits that help raise immunity, provide tissue repair, and wound recuperation. They may have anti-fungal and anti-bacterial properties. They can be dried and turned into a powder (hence 'powdered super vegetables'). What this means is that sea vegetables, such as kelp and chlorella are great meals. Although I was listing sea vegetables as number ten, they should possibly be the number one survival food in this top ten list. The purpose once more is that fresh produce is likely to be in short supply or disappear completely in several regions during an extensive emergency.

Even the best survival foods can go bad

Remember, many non-perishable meals including several indexed here do not have a long shelf life, often just months. You will want to have a system in place to "rotate" your non-perishable meals before than they expire: when non-perishable food nears its expiration date, either eat it or perhaps donate it to a local food bank (food banks generally serve food shortly after donation). Then, buy new non-perishable food and put it in your emergency meals storage. With a tool like this in place, if a catastrophe strikes, you will have a supply of non-perishable ingredients for at least the first few months after the catastrophe, and you or your family should not have to rely solely on freeze-dried food, like many people are stocking up on nowadays.

Just because you have stocked up does not mean you are prepared

If you have a good stockpile of meals going and you are rotating as needed to keep your emergency stores ready to be eat, that does not mean you are ready for a true disaster. Having everything stocked up and ready at home is fantastic, but what if you are away from home when a real survival situation takes place? All your research and stockpiling means nothing if you cannot get to it. That's why you need to even have a get-home bag. A get- home bag is exactly what it looks like – it is a backpack with a few emergency supplies that must be sufficient to get you home safe in the event of a catastrophic or dangerous event.

Your get-home bag needs to (as much as possible) go where you go. This means keeping it in the trunk of your vehicle when you go to work, taking it with you if you go on vacation, and other situations. The get-home bag is the bridge to get you from wherever you are when disaster strikes to the safety of your house, where you have already organized emergency supplies and survival equipment. If you do not have an appropriate survival backpack to prepare your get-home bag, make sure you read our guide about the best survival backpacks and pick one of the top options.

Caution about "food fatigue"

When getting ready for an emergency, you must remember bulk freeze-dried emergency foods that have a shelf life of several years. Please note that it isn't always the best idea to purchase freeze-dried meals, though. The reason is food fatigue.

Are you able to imagine what it would be like to eat freeze-dried meals every day, month after month, in a time of prolonged catastrophe? Not only can packaged, processed foods be harder on someone's health (due to meals additives and preservatives, high cholesterol, sodium, and more). However, it may also get very boring after a while.

In a time of the prolonged disaster, having a bag of M&Ms, smoked pork jerky, or maybe a soda can sometimes make a huge improvement on morale, especially if you have children. With that said, do not discount the value in having bulk freeze-dried meals stocked up for your pantry, particularly if you would like to help friends and other family members who have supplies. Leading manufacturers such as the Wise Company (with its wide variety) and Mountain House (with its classic bucket) factor in food fatigue and include of variety intentionally, and as such, they arrive with many flavorful options for you and your family.

Fresh cuts of meat aren't the best survival food, but

One last issue to touch upon: people stocking up on the best survival meals would possibly skip the beef aisle altogether, believing that cuts of meat will expire quickly in an emergency.

What do you have in your freezer at home right now?

Build yourself an outside smoker. That is how early civilizations prepared meat for long-term storage. So, take into account as a "Plan B" for your frozen meat in the event of a power outage, where the power is down for good.

Ways to Purify Water in the Wilderness

Straw-type filters are one of the most common styles of water filters used to purify water in a wilderness survival scenario. There are a number of those in the marketplace, which include the LifeStraw. These filters work by blocking anything that is larger than 0.2 microns. Since most bacteria are larger than 2 microns, that's a pretty good protection margin. The LifeStraw will filter out up to 1,000 liters of water.

Straw-type filters are used by putting one end directly In the stream or lake and drinking with the straw. This is very handy; however, it does not help you in purifying water to take with you in a canteen or water bottle.

When you research straw-type filters, there are important things to look for, the filtration size (the 0.2 microns above) and the number of gallons of water that the filter is good for. Some straws do not filter out as finely or as many gallons that the LifeStraw will.

Purify water in the wasteland with bag-type water filters

Many people carry a bag-type filter in their bug-out bag as well. The main advantage of a bag-type filter over a straw-types that the water you run through the bag-type can then be placed into a canteen or water bottle to take with you and drink later. That is important because it allows you to move away from the water as you are traveling.

LifeStraw also makes a bag-kind filter, even though it does not actually use a bag. In this case, the bag is a hard plastic cup; however, the idea is the same. Because it uses the same filter out as the other LifeStraw, it offers you an equal level of safety. Another first-rate filter is the Sawyer Mini Water Filtration System, which uses a hollow fiber design. Their design filters less finely at 0.1 microns, but may last longer, since the filter can be used for a 100,000 gallons of water.

Using water purification tablets

Iodine is a bit inconvenient to carry with you. Instead, people use iodine pills, which include those by Potable Aqua. These are easy to work with and offer a convenient way to purify water in the wilderness. The biggest problem with depending on tablets of this kind is that, eventually, you run out, leaving you without a way of purifying water.

To use the pills, a canteen or water bottle is filled with water and the tablets inserted. These are amazing for an emergency situation, keeping them in a survival kit, but you could not use them for long-term water purification.

You could accomplish a similar effect using ordinary household bleach. Bleach is chlorine, the same substance that is used in municipal water towers and for keeping pathogens from growing in swimming pools. The trick is finding a container to carry the bleach in, so that it won't leak out all over your food and other supplies. You will need an eye dropper as well, as you need to add eight drops of bleach to each gallon of water to purify it. Like the iodine tablets, give the bleach a half-hour to kill off any pathogens.

Purify water in the wilderness through boiling

You may also kill the pathogens in water by boiling it. This requires having some sort of container, such as a canteen cup, which won't melt or burn in a fireplace. In a pinch, you could make a cup out of birch-bark and boil the water in it. So long as the flames are kept below the bottom of the cup, the cup won't burn.

Purify water in the wild through solar power

A water pasteurization indicator, or WAPI, can be used for purifying water by using solar power. Put the WAPI in the water. Lay the bottle somewhere that it is in direct sunlight, ideally somewhere where it is on a black or dark-colored surface.

The sun will heat the water in the bottle sufficiently to reach the pasteurization temperature. You will know that it is warm enough because the wax pellet in the WAPI will soften.

You should be cautious while drinking the water though, ensuring that your lips do not touch any part of the outside of the bottle, other than what is covered by the bottle cap.

Yes, over-hydration could cause issues, but you need enough water in your body for your organs to function. The trouble is, you do not always have the option to carry potable water with you (or you can run out).

1. Boiling

The easiest way to purify water is to boil it, provided you have the system to do so, plus a campfire or camp range. Place water in a pot over high heat until you have rolling bubbles, and let them roll for at least five minutes. Then, allow it cool before drinking, or you will burn your lips and tongue.

2. Filtration or purification pumps

If you visit a camping and outdoors supply store, you will surely find many great styles of pumps with filters and purifiers to make sure non-potable water goes in, but drinkable water comes out - right into your water bottle. This is executed by way of pushing water through a ceramic or charcoal filter and treating it with chemical compounds.

Some high-tech water bottles have this system built into them so that you do not need to pump water into a separate container; the purification process takes place as you squeeze or suck water directly into your mouth.

3. Purification drops and drugs

A simple and less expensive - however, not necessarily the best tasting - approach of purifying water is by using purification drops. The most common chemical used is iodine, but chlorine or potassium permanganate are also effective. Allow the chemicals to sit the water for at least 20 minutes before drinking, and blend it with powdered mixes to mask any of its flavors.

4. Get water from the ground

All the previous strategies require you to carry water or have a water supply close by - however, what if you don't have any?

You can pull moisture out of the earth by digging a hole in the ground and placing a container on the bottom. Cover the hole with plastic so that no moisture escapes, and put a small weight (like a rock) in the middle of the cover so there is a dip in the middle. When the water evaporates from the ground upwards, it condenses on the cover and drips down into the bucket.

Of course, this approach is not the quickest way to get potable water, so just try to do not remember to carry some. However, in case of an emergency, remember this technique - on the side of a box and a few types of a plastic cover.

The Mind of Survival

The work of surviving outdoors does not begin with lighting a fire or constructing a shelter. Before any of those, you need to develop first the mindset of a true survivor. Attempt to find a real life survival story, and you will find that these survivors have similar mental tendencies which allow them to endure the tough conditions they have been in.

Growing a survivor's mindset is extremely crucial, and below are the top five traits that you will need:

1. Positive attitude

Just because nearly all survival guides are preaching about the importance of having a great mindset does not mean that you need to think about it as another cliché. A great mindset is an actual necessity. This is also one of the most difficult abilities to master, but it is going to be worth the trouble. Practice this mindset each day and you will be ready if you ever find yourself lost in the wilderness.

2. Motivation

What's the only thing that motivates someone to stay alive even when things have gone wrong? A variety of survival memoirs discuss the survivor's devotion to their non-secular beliefs or a higher power for supplying hope and motivation. Other survivors have also discussed their important choice to return to their loved ones, friends, and family. What do you believe will inspire you to stay alive during a survival emergency? That is for you to decide as it differs for every person.

3. Mental strength

This is not about bodily prowess, stamina, pain tolerance, or the number of calluses you have. Mental strength is your willpower as well as your mind's endurance. With the goal to be mentally strong, you need to suffer through the unbearable, tolerate the insupportable, and overpower your choice to surrender and all your weaknesses.

4. Adaptability

Survival and adaptability go hand-in-hand. Consider the survival of animals and plants. Those who failed to adapt to the changing environment did not survive. Those that changed and evolved managed to live on. You want to adapt to all the changing environments, situations, and events. You should know which things you should keep and those that should be abandoned.

5. Work Ethic

Your work ethic is another major element of your survival mindset. Being in a hard situation often teaches people to work harder and better the future, assuming that there will be future. A true survivor is one that has a strong work ethic, a person who doesn't give up. Your strong work ethic could actually go a long way to make up for things that you weren't able to be lucky enough to have.

Chapter 11: Before Shtf

The first psychological link between preppers around the globe is thinking ahead and being ready for anything. So many people talk about situations like zombie apocalypses they see on TV, an **Outbreak-**style pandemic, or huge storms and then dismiss them by saying, "But that won't happen!" While a zombie apocalypse is not the biggest concern for preppers, situations like pandemics and major weather events are, and they are not as unlikely as most people have deluded themselves into thinking. How quickly society forgets about SARS, the bird flu, and more recently, ebola. People tend to get a little worried at the time of an event like this, but when their countries or even just their little areas are spared, they feel invincible. Even if they do take the event as a wake-up call, few ever do anything about it. Few people actually start preparing in case another wave of disease sweeps through.

The same goes for weather events. If a person is not on the coast, they are not overly concerned about tsunamis or major flooding, but drought, famine, snow, and rain affect (and include) the regions not close to the ocean. Just because Hollywood has not made an epic movie about a decade-long drought does not mean it could not happen. Remember the Dust Bowl? Thousands of North American farmers found their once-fertile soil turned to dust and tried to find different work, only to find that the Great Depression had annihilated all other employment. Some regions suffered from extreme drought for up to eight years. Preppers are not nutcases for imagining scenarios where one's chances of survival depended upon self-reliance and good forethought. The scenarios they are thinking of have already happened or are currently happening in other places in the world.

Another important part of pre-SHTF thinking is actually taking action. The best preppers will not only be aware of the possible scenarios, but they will have an organized plan of attack. This means stockpiling. The psychology here is stockpiling what one needs for those oh-so-likely situations like power outages due to thunderstorms and for those not-so-likely-but-still-possible situations like the complete collapse of society after nuclear war. Preppers have lists. Lots of lists. Their families' lives depend on them having good lists and good stockpiles. This means enough water and ways to create good water, like water filters and tablets. This means food that will last for a long time, like canned meats, fruits, and veggies. This means items that can be used to barter for more essentials when the stockpile starts to get low. It also means learning skills like carpentry, first aid, hunting, and even beekeeping. These services can be bartered and are also essential for long-term societal collapse. Good prepper thinking is not overly influenced by the latest fads or expensive prepper "must-haves," but is grounded in reliable research and a keen awareness of the needs of their families.

Good prepper thinking also factors in different responses to a SHTF scenario. One will not always be able to stay at home and hunker down. There may be a time when it becomes too dangerous to stay where you are and bugging out becomes the best option. The best preppers will have bug-out bags ready with a few days' worth of essentials (food, medical supplies, defense) so they can move quickly, and, most importantly, a plan about where they are going. Bugging out is extremely dangerous if you do not have a safe place to escape to. To prepare your family, hold some drills like many do with fires or tornados. This will help young children especially get used to the idea of leaving suddenly and urgently. If you do not have drills and suddenly have to leave everything, your child will be in completely shock and likely terrified. If he or she has some experience with it, it will be much less traumatic.

While a big part of prepper thinking is based on self-reliance, a good prepper also knows not to make enemies and to develop relationships with people they can trust. There is no strength quite like strength in numbers, and if your house becomes a war zone of violent looters trying to get in, you will want to know your neighbor has got your back. These relationships are also important for bartering. Bartering is not something preppers do with everyone, because lots of people might use the opportunity to scope out what supplies you have and where you are keeping them. Develop relationships that are mutually beneficial. This kind of advance thinking is definite of good preppers. Always think ahead and always be ready.

Chapter 12: Packing A Bug Out Bag

For Your Whole Family

If you're simply bugging out by yourself, then it's going to be rather straightforward in putting together a bug out bag.

But if you're bugging out with your entire family, and particularly if you have children in your family, then you're going to have to make a bug out bag or bug out bags that are suitable for everyone and includes the specific thing that your children will need.

In this chapter, we'll talk about how to pack a bug out bag for your whole family including if you have to bug out with infants and toddlers, elementary aged children, and middle schoolers and teenagers.

INFANTS AND TODDLERS

If you have to bug out with infants and toddlers, obviously they won't be able to carry anything with them. On the contrary, you'll have to carry them. You'll also have to be prepared to deal with how they react to a new environment or the situation that's happening around them; it can be very easy for an infant or toddler to become upset and distressed by what's happening.

As a result, you're going to have to tend to your infant and toddler very often in order to care for their needs. You also need to take their weight into account in regards to how many items you put into your bug out bag.

A major issue that infant and toddlers can bring in a survival situation is noise. If they become distressed by what's going on, their cries can gain the attention of unwanted visitors. This is why you must carry additional items in your bug out bag that tend to the needs of your infant or toddler and can help keep them quiet in a critical scenario.

Some additional items to carry in your bug out bag if you have an infant or toddler include:

-Formula: just as you would carry real food for the rest of your family, infants and toddlers need to be given plenty of formula for them to feed on.

-Pacifier: a pacifier will help keep your infant or toddler calm and quiet and even help them sleep better at night when things will be more uncomfortable.

-Diapers: this should be an obvious thing to include if you have infants or toddlers with you. Reusable ones will be better, since they can also be applied to other survival related purposes as well.

ELEMENTARY SCHOOL AGED CHILDREN

If you have any children in your family who are in elementary school (ages 4-11) they can begin to take part in your family's prepping tasks. While they won't be old enough to assume major responsibilities, they can easily help find firewood, forage for edible plants, or fish with adult supervision.

Elementary school aged children will be able to carry smaller packs with them that contain essential survival items along with some personal items to keep them happy such as toys that are not powered by batteries. They won't be old enough to carry actual backpacks or personal bug out bags, but they can carry small packs slung across their shoulder with very basic items. You will want to make sure that they are fully trained in the use of each item; not only for safety reasons, but because the skills that you teach them now will stick with them for the rest of your life.

Your children will need to be kept entertained in the evenings or while you're setting up camp, so including a couple of simple toys for them in your bug out bag isn't a bad idea. Make sure that the children choose which toys they want in the bag.

At the same time, children these ages will have significantly less stamina than middle schoolers and teenagers, so be prepared to carry them at some point.

MIDDLE SCHOOLERS AND TEENAGERS

Middle school aged children and teenagers will be far easier to have with you in a bug out situation because they actually understand the danger and risk of a bugging out situation, and furthermore, are ready to begin assuming major responsibilities.

All children in your family ages 12 and up needs to carry their own bug out bag with their own gear. Their backpack shouldn't be as large as yours, but it should be of equal quality. Examples of items that needs to be included in their bag include items that will help them complete the following tasks:

-First Aid

-Signaling and Navigation

-Fire Making

-Self-Defense

-Scavenging

-Hunting, Trapping, and Foraging

-Shelter Construction

-Water Purification

In other words, whereas before you would have to carry items for your younger children, when it comes to middle schoolers and teenagers they should easily be able to carry their own items. In addition, they should also be easily able to assume larger responsibilities as they begin the transition to adulthood.

Make sure that your teens fully understand the gravities of the situation and why their help in your family's survival efforts are absolutely critical. Teens need to understand that survival is a challenge, but they also need to understand that is an easily conquerable one if they have the right gear and the right skills. They can also help you in caring for or comforting the smaller children in your family if you have any.

Having to bug out with your entire family is undeniably going to make an already complicated situation even more complicated. However, it is not anything that can't be overcome. You need to think very carefully about what you put into your bug out bag and follow the advice that we have learned. Remember that infants and toddlers need to be given items to help keep them calm and quiet in a disaster scenario while middle schooled children and teenagers are ready to begin assuming survival responsibilities and carry their own bug out bags. . .

Remember that only you know your family and your children, so if there are any additional items or precautions that you feel you need to include, be sure that you do.

Chapter 13: First Steps

We all have to start somewhere and that is right from the beginning with the basics. You can not jump straight in to the deep end without first understanding what it takes to survive.

What are You Prepping For?

Let us first take a step back and think about what we are preparing for in the first place. There are no right or wrong answers to this. My reasons may be completely different to yours.

No prepper can truly prepare for everything, it is impossible. Disasters are happening every day in some part of the world be it volcanoes, tornadoes, flooding, earthquakes or something completely different. Every area is prone to different disasters and you need to look in to the history of your own area in order to prioritize the events that you most need to prepare for.

This being said, there are also a number of man-made disasters that may impact you such as terrorism, riots, chemical spills, and war to name a few. There are also personal emergencies such as kidnapping, unemployment, financial disaster, and your home being burned down.

These are all real emergencies that you need to think about. Once you have a clear understanding as to the types of disasters that you want to prepare for, it will make it a hell of a lot easier to get started.

The media and the government would like us to believe that we are completely safe and many believe them, however, the yearly death tolls from disasters do not lie like the media and the government. You can not continue with the belief that the government will fix everything when you need them. You need to be wise and prepare for the unexpected.

The Rule of Three

It does not take a rocket scientist to understand that without such things as water, food, and air, we just wont survive. This is why we live by the understanding of the rule of threes. These are as follows:

Three minutes without air

Three hours without shelter

Three days without water

Three weeks without food

Three months without hope

There are no amount of preparations that can deal with air and hope but shelter, water, and food, we can do something about. Following a disaster, shelter comes out on top, this is your first priority but it might not necessarily mean exactly what you think it means.

Walls and a roof over your head are all good but when there are no structures left standing, shelter is any means of keeping clean and maintaining a healthy body temperature. We need heat, fire creates heat and this falls under the shelter rule, as does any means of keeping clean such as a portable shower. As for the water, where would you and everybody else go when the faucets stop working or something happens to the local water source? A good prepper always understands the need for clean water.

Create a Family Emergency Plan

The idea of the family emergency plan is to enable you to work together with your family to write down all the information on what you and each family member would need to do in the event of an emergency. This plan should not just be made for major disasters but also for little emergencies that can happen as you go about your day.

Below are some things that you should consider when working with your family to create your emergency plan.

Identify the locations of gas, water and electricity supplies and ensure that each member of the family understands how to turn them off.

Make sure that every member of the family understands the escape routes of the home in case of a fire. This should include how to get out if the doors are blocked.

Identify safe meeting places where the family will gather if it is unsafe to return home. This should include a local place and a place that is farther away. Be sure to include all addresses and telephone numbers.

Include a list of all contact numbers such as relatives, schools, friends, doctors, work, local authority, and utility company.

Details of household insurance.

Details of any medications that may be needed by family members.

Each member of the family should receive a copy of the family emergency plan and one should be placed within the home where everybody can easily see it.

Chapter 14: Medical Supplies And Emergency Equipment

Aside from essential food and water supplies, you'll also need basic medical supplies to treat a wide range of ailments and injuries. If you live in a region where natural disasters are probable, or if you predict social or economic upheaval, stock up on these supplies at the beginning of your prepping schedule.

First Aid Kit

An old tool box, fishing tackle box, or Tupperware will make an excellent carrying case for a first aid kit. A plastic box is a better option because it will be keep the contents of your first aid kit dry. If you are concerned about the contents getting wet because of heavy rain or flooding, secure your container with duct tape. Also, it's crucial that you inspect your first aid kit regularly to keep it well-maintained and fully stocked.

A basic first aid kit should be stored as a bare minimum when prepping for a SHTF or disaster scenario. This kit should include supplies for caring for wounds (such as bandages), antibiotic ointments to treat infections, over-the-counter drugs such as painkillers, cold and flu relief, cough syrup, anti-nausea pills, allergy medication, and anti-diarrheal medications, such as salt solutions. It is recommended to compile a more comprehensive first aid kit however, which includes the items listed below.

In terms of medicines and solutions, ensure to stock the following:

Hydrogen peroxide to wash and disinfect wounds

Wet wipes or anti-bacterial wipes

Antibiotic ointment

Individually wrapped alcohol swabs

Aspirin and non-aspirin tablets

Prescriptions and any long-term medications (keep these current)

Diarrhoea medicine

Eye drops

Also, remember to stock a range of dressings, including:

Bandage strips

Ace bandages

Rolled gauze

Cotton-tipped swabs

Adhesive tape

Other first aid supplies include:

First aid manual

Scissors

Tweezers

Thermometer

Bar of soap

Wet wipes and nappies for babies

Tissues

Sunscreen

Paper cups

Pocket knife

Small plastic bags

Safety pins

Needle and thread

Instant cold packs for sprains

Sanitary napkins

Splinting materials

Remember to keep crucial medications, including vaccinations, refrigerated if possible. If this is not possible because of a power outage or a lack of equipment, keep medications in a cool, dry, and dark location away from direct sunlight. Do not use medications if you are in doubt about the expiry date.

Special medical items

Always consider the needs of your entire group when preparing medical supplies. Perhaps a member of your group is diabetic and requires a regular supply of insulin, or perhaps you will be caring for pensioners or babies, who may need specialist medication. Also, make sure you have adequate sanitary supplies for women, including tampons and sanitary towels. If you are unsure of the medical requirements of your group, ask for further details before it's too late.

Personal Hygiene

Although it may not seem critical to your survival in SHTF situation, hygiene is imperative to prevent illness and the spread of disease. This becomes particularly important if the disaster is a hurricane or a flood. If you are low on clean water, and it's impossible to boil it or disinfect the water using the aforementioned methods from the last chapter, try to source some alcohol-based sanitizer for washing your hands. While it does not guarantee to kill all germs, it can quickly and sufficiently kill many but you must try to rinse off visible dirt before application. Also, in terms of personal hygiene you may want to have sponges, tooth brushes and plenty of toilet paper in your survival kit, if not to fight tooth-decay and cleanliness, at least for personal comfort!

Emergency Equipment

While prepping it's important to consider any possible outcome, including fires, flooding, and storm damage. To help prepare for these scenarios, stock a fire extinguisher and breathing apparatus. Gas masks or respirators will be absolutely crucial if you predict a threat of poisonous gases such as smoke inhalation or potential explosions of toxic materials. Ensure that you have multiple pieces of breathing apparatus for everyone in your group, and always apply your own mask first before attending to others. If it's the case you are preparing for a nuclear attack, you will need protective HEV suits and you should consider retreating to a lead-lined nuclear bunker.

Power

Power Outages

Often, a natural disaster or SHTF scenario will threaten your power supply, leaving you without lights, heating, operative cooking equipment, and the ability to operate and charge cell phones, batteries, and other electronic devices. Even if you have adequate food and water supplies, disruptions to your power supply will affect your morale and will make your experience much more challenging.

Preparing for power outages is a crucial component of survival prepping. You may think disasters will never happen, yet it's difficult to deny that storms and extreme weather conditions often leave people without power, especially those living in areas prone to storms, or natural disasters such as hurricanes and earthquakes. Even if your area isn't affected by extreme weather, electrical outages do happen, often at peak times when electricity is in high demand. If you are well prepared for a power outage, trust that you'll be much better equipped to cope with other emergency situations, including quarantines, loss of income or belongings, civil unrest, and economic collapse.

Remember, if the power goes out for a long period, you may be unable to leave your home if downed power lines are obstructing your exit. Stay well clear of these. Also, if the power is out in your home it's likely that street lighting will be out too and it may be dangerous to leave. If power outages are short, from a few hours to a few days, the best plan is to stay put and to depend on the prepared supplies you will have in place. Only if power outages occur for longer periods will you have to start thinking about alternative sources of power.

Heat and Light Alternatives

When the power goes out, your top priorities are protecting your food, water, and medical supplies from excessive heat and making suitable plans against exposure to extreme temperatures. If the power outage occurs during winter, in a cold climate, staying warm is crucial. To retain heat, block off a single room in which all of the group occupy. Keep the door closed and place a towel or blanket at the foot of the door to reduce heat loss. Dress in layers and wear a hat, scarf, and gloves (fingerless gloves are good if you still need to use your hands).

Initially, layering up and reducing heat loss should keep your warm, but soon enough you'll need an alternative heat source (depending on the climate). If you have a fireplace or a woodstove in your house, remember to keep at least three days worth of fuel, firelighters, and matches close to hand. If not, a propane or oil heater is the next best thing. You can also use other stoves such as hexamine or gas stoves to warm up but these will be much less efficient since they are designed for cooking. To prevent the build-up of carbon monoxide, use generators, pressure washers, grills, hexamine and camping stoves outdoors or where there is suitable ventilation. If this is a concern, it may be worth investing in a carbon monoxide detector, which will alert you to the presence of the gas before it reaches dangerous levels.

When it comes to lighting, darkness can make calm situations seem more frightening and stressful. Make sure you have a working flashlight with spare batteries, in a place you can easily access when it's dark. Also stock long-burning candles and waterproof matches alongside your flashlight. Ensure that matches are stored in a waterproof container such as a sealable food bag or Tupperware. A kerosene lamp can also be useful. If you decide to prep your premises, garden stake solar lights and a hand crank or solar lantern are wise choices, allowing you to generate power without the use of electricity.

Generating Your Own Power

When the power goes out there are inexpensive and ingenious ways to generate your own power. Rather than investing in an expensive engine generator, here are some other ideas.

Batteries can be made easily and inexpensively and can be used to power lights, heaters, engines, and a whole range of electrical devices. To make a simple 1.5V battery you'll need a bar of copper, a bar of aluminum, a piece of copper wire, some bleach, and a container full of water. Aluminum can be salvaged from used soda cans, while copper can be found in the wiring in houses and in cars. Also, you can use aluminum cans for water containers, providing the bars do not touch the edges of the can. Once you've sourced your materials, place the copper and the aluminum bars in the water and connect them with the copper wire. Then pour roughly a teaspoon of bleach into the water. The more bleach you add, the more amps are produced and the faster the bars will corrode.

To generate 12 volts of DC electricity, which is often enough to power electrical lights and tools, you'll need 8-9 small batteries connected in a series. As an example, the headlights in cars run on a 12 volt DC current. Bear in mind that typically, lighting in houses runs on AC current, rather than DC. When scavenging for electrical devices keep a look out for DC, as AC appliances will be useless with these batteries unless you have a converter. To connect batteries in a series, simply connect the positive post (copper) to the can of the next battery using copper wire. Note, a simple amp meter is a useful addition to your supplies since it allows you to test the output of your batteries.

Other ways to generate your own power include gasoline generators, homemade wind turbines and other renewable sources, which will be more reliable for long term survival, especially if infrastructure is damaged and it seems unlikely to recover. Other renewable sources of power include solar, hydro-electric, and tidal power.

Chapter 15: How To Stock Food Items

You can stock the food items using five procedures: canning, freezing, fermenting, dehydrating and curing and smoking.

If you want to **can foods**, then divide them in acidic and non-acidic categories first. The acidic foods like tomatoes need to processed in the boiling water first and then kept in a good quality pressure canner that needs to be cooled according to the instructions on its manual. As for meat and veggies, make sure to process them at a ten pound pressure at the sea level. Canned food normally lasts for a year. From the above explanation, it is clear that there are 2 canning methods depending on the acidity of the foods that you want to can (the links will show you more information on how to go about it).

Water bath canning

Pressure canning

To **freeze foods**, boil them and keep them in Ziploc bags after treating the bags with a vacuum sealer. They can last for around six to twelve months.

For **dehydrating foods**, you need to a good quality food dehydrator and then dehydrate the food and store it in Ziploc bags. Dehydrated foods are good for about one year.

To **cure and smoke foods**, you should cure meats and steaks using a cure mixture containing nitrates and then smoke them on a grill. You can then refrigerate or freeze these foods for up to six months.

To **ferment foods** such as fruits and veggies, clean the foods and then keep them in cider vinegar or vinegar with five percent acidity, and refrigerate it. Fermented foods remain in good condition for around six months.

Make sure to follow all these guidelines strictly to ensure that your bug-out bag contains what you truly need to stay alive.

Tip: You will also need to stock items to be used for skinning animals that you may hunt in the wild.

Note: The basic idea behind proper food storage is to keep it away from moisture, oxygen and to ensure that it is properly sealed from pests and other hazards.

Note: Avoid spoilage of food by using the FIFO method of using up food in your pantry. You shouldn't just wait for food to spoil just because it is in your survival pantry; you can come up with an effective rotation plan that will ensure that you eat whatever is in the pantry while restocking it in the process such that you ensure that you always have fresh food in your pantry.

Now that you have sufficient information on how to prep for shelter, water and food, the next bit is building up your survival kit and bug out bag.

How to Prepare the Ultimate Supply Kit

You cannot estimate for how long you would have to live through a calamity and when a SHTF (shit hits the fan) situation will take place. You cannot also estimate how harsh a disaster can be and the problems it can bring with itself, but the wisest move on your part is to prepare in advance for it and that too, like a pro. Providing prepping guidance for over a decade now has enabled me to help hundreds of people prepare successfully for different catastrophes, so I can help you do the same too.

You need to start by preparing your ultimate supply kit. This kit will contain a number of items that will help you manage yourself and bear the harsh conditions of the environment in case a disaster strikes.

What is the Ultimate Supply Kit?

According to FEMA (Federal Emergency Management Agency), you must make preparations for at least two weeks to endure an emergency. You must have water and food that can help you live for a minimum of two weeks, and you need to prepare three kits. Yes, one for your vehicle, another for your house and a third one for your workplace, so you can grab your bug out bag and escape the calamity from wherever you are.

I know you must be stressing right now because stocking food and survival supplies for about two weeks would seem expensive to you. Well, the good news is that you don't have to buy all the supplies in one go. The economical way to prep is to gradually accumulate the emergency supplies, so you don't experience the harsh financial burn. Buy a few items each week, so you can prepare the ultimate survival kit, also referred to as the out bag or bug-out bag in a period of two to three months.

Although you need to stock for at least two weeks, you might have to stock more items for certain members of your family. Items must be stored according to the gender, special needs, and medical conditions of each family member. So, if a person needs more water, or cannot survive without certain vitamins, then you must prepare for them accordingly.

What to Focus on First

Your first focus needs to be on shelter and water, and then food. This is because you can survive for only three hours without the right body temperature, three days without drinking any water and about three weeks without food. This means that whenever you get stuck in a chaotic situation or a natural disaster attacks your area, your first priority needs to be providing a moderate temperature environment for yourself and your family along with water.

We have already discussed these items; simply revisit them to learn more on how to prep sufficiently for them.

To make it easier for you, follow the following guidelines depending on the topography:

Shelter

*Tarp – You can use this as a canopy, a blanket or even a ground-sheet

*Bivi Bag – A waterproof and a compacted survival bag

*Sleeping Bag – A roll in waterproof bag

*Tent –Use this in case there is sufficient space

*Bothy Bag – A temporary tent shelter

*Foil Blanket – A waterproof and heat-reflecting shelter

Food

*Ration Heaters – For heating frozen meals

*Energy Tablets - Sweets tablets for instant infusion of energy

*Survival rations - Survival meals

Tools

*Saw – Use this for cutting wood and plastic sheets

*Crowbar – Use this for opening jammed windows and doors

*Small shovel – For digging mud, debris

*Multipurpose tool – This should take care of any cutting, repairing and sawing

*Knife – Ensure it has a sharp blade for precise cutting

*Axe – For splitting wood

Fire starters

*Flint – Can create sparks under every weather

*Matches – A weatherproof option

*Lighter - A windproof option

*Candles – Also a light source

*Tinder – Can start a fire under every condition

Light

*Hand Torch – For signaling via lighting

*Light Sticks – One time use glow sticks

*Backup Torch - A pen torch

*Head Torch - For keeping your hands free

Navigation / signaling

*Satellite device – Satellite phone or tracker

*Bright red blanket – This is for signaling and warmth

*Mirror –This is for signaling and camping

*Compass – This one helps in finding directions

*Whistle – This should be without pea design that won't freeze

*Beacon - Waterproof flashlight for signaling

Water

*Water Storage – A water bag, or a bottle

*Purification Straw – Purifies free flowing water

*Filtration bottle – For treating all kinds of water

*Water Purification Tablets – This one purifies stored water

Heating / cooking

*Solid fuel kettle – If space is ample

*Aluminum Foil - For minimal cooking

*Mess Tins – For heating and cooking on campfire

*Hexi Stove – Micro stove run by solid fuel

*Fuel – According to the stove

Repairing

*Duct tape – Use this for fixing anything

*Cable ties – This is for repairing and binding

*Nylon utility cord – Multipurpose cord

*Fishing line –This is for fishing

*Steel or Brass wire – This is for snaring/repairing

*Sewing Needle with thread

First aid

*Sun protection - sunscreen cream or lotion

*Insect protector – Insect repellents and coverings

*Wound closing plasters - Adhesive plasters

*First Aid kit – For treating minor injuries

*Haemostatic powder - To prevent excessive bleeding

*Suction pump – for sucking venom after stings

*Burns dressings – For protecting and soothing burns

*SAM Splint – For immobilizing limbs

Power

*Solar charger – It can charge batteries or devices directly

*Emergency charger - For mobile and/or other devices

*Alkaline batteries – AA or AAA

*Lithium batteries - For cold weather

Communication

*Satellite phone – Voice messages with location details

*Radio – This will help you listen to news broadcasts even with power cuts

*Walkie talkie –This should help with free communication

First Aid Kit

It is essential to keep a first aid kit in your survival kit as well, so you can treat injuries promptly and prevent infections from exacerbating. Keep the following items in your bug-out bag. For starters, it is best to start stocking for up to two weeks, but initially, you should triple the quantity of all the items, so they can help you endure harsh calamities for up to a month or two.

Antacid: Keep them to help relive tummy aches. Stock about ten packs of antacids.

Aspirin or a Pain Reliever without Aspirin: It will help you get relief from body pains and headaches. Keep about ten packs of these too.

Stool Softeners: These come in handy when you become constipated due to a lack of water or fiber consumption, or any other factor. Keep about five packs of these.

Kleenex: Stock about 100 packs of Kleenex or any other tissue paper.

Feminine Hygiene Supplies. Buy these in a quantity that can last for at least two months.

Band-aids: Stock at least 200 band-aids in different sizes.

Disposable Wipes: Stock around 500 of these.

Antibiotic Ointment: Make sure to store at least 20 tubes of 100g good quality antibiotic ointment. Buy one that suits all the family members and make sure to keep the allergies of different members into account when making this purchase.

Prescription Medicines: Buy at least two weeks of these medications.

Reading Glasses: If you or family member wears them, then do stock an additional pair of these as well.

Make sure to keep all these items in a clean, waterproof bag and replace the medications with new ones if they expire.

Note: Different situations will require different items in your survival bag. You can keep all these items in your bug out bag.

So what is it you should keep in your first aid kit?

Chapter 16: Misconceptions About Prepping And Survival

These notions about preppers are wrong!

There are many common misconceptions about prepping and survival. Those who do not understand why you do this may hold some of these misconceptions. This is why many preppers do not like discussing prepping with non-preppers. Let's clear the air a little:

Preppers are Paranoid

If people believe that preppers are unnecessarily paranoid, this means half the American population is paranoid. Regardless, being prepared just means that you would be more confident in the uncertainty life may bring you. Instead of always worrying about unforeseen circumstances, preppers may actually become more stable and balanced. Prepping reduces the fear and panic a person has of the uncertainties brought about by a crisis.

Prepping is for the Rich

It is true that prepping would cost you a significant amount of cash, but it is equally false that prepping is for the rich. There are levels of prepping; the most basic prepping endeavors are generally affordable for the average person. The consolation to prepping is the fact that money doesn't deter us from investing in safety protocols for our family and loved ones.

Preppers Live in Isolation

Preppers do not leave in isolation; they could be your friends, siblings, co-worker and even neighbor next door. Many do not live in bunkers, woods, or secluded places;

preppers live a "normal life" by most definitions.

Preppers are Irrational

A school of thought believes that preppers are irrational with their thoughts because they anticipate an apocalypse. I would like to reemphasize that preparing for an apocalypse is not all there is to prepping. An apocalypse may be the ultimate worst-case scenario that a prepper might think of after fulfilling all the lower levels of prepping. There are many other emergency scenarios that you have to account for, such as earthquakes, war, famine and a viral outbreak.

At the end of the day, those who live the prepping lifestyle would be better equipped to handle a crisis, and should the unthinkable happen, they could be among the survivors.

In addition to misconceptions about preppers, there are many myths about survival. Here we would explore some of them:

72 Hours Would Do for an Emergency Plan

This myth has no factual backing; by experience, we know that most emergencies, disasters, or catastrophic experiences are not short-lived. They may extend for up to a week or more. Most times, preppers are advised to have an emergency plan for at least a two-week period.

You Can Depend on the Government in Times of Crisis

As much you wish you could count on the government for your security and safety, in the event of a disaster, you might have to depend on yourself. Catastrophic events usually result in millions of people seeking help from the government. In some cases, the government may not have been prepared for the crisis.

Besides, the government system can never be perfect as long as people are in charge of the offices. Some government employees will also be affected by a crisis, and they may be faced with hard choices. So, let the government be your last or backup option when you have exhausted all other means of survival.

Being A Loner Equals Survival

This is another survival myth; in reality, being in a group gives you much better odds of surviving a crisis. A community may provide much-needed help and assistance in your areas of deficiency. You do not have the luxury of being an island of knowledge, and you may not have been prepared beyond the basic level.

With a community of people, the stress that comes with emergencies is evenly distributed with more people. For instance, imagine having to protect yourself and sleep at the same time in the wild! In contrast, members of a group could take turns performing tasks so that no one becomes mentally and emotionally drained.

Misunderstanding of Natural Phenomena

In your bid to survive, you must be careful not to misunderstand some natural phenomena. For example, you may be wrong to assume that birds are always headed in the direction of the water. Trying to follow their trails or path may land you in bigger trouble. You need discretion and instincts to make some survival decisions. Remember to always plan and reevaluate. Sometimes survival is about trusting your instincts when you have not fully prepared for the scenario.

Forging Ahead Equals Survival

Forging ahead does not always guarantee survival. It depends on the nature of the crisis. You should get going only when there is a clear need to proceed from your location. The more you roam about, the more you would expose yourself to dangers. Preppers recommend that you stay put in a safe place, and only forge ahead when there is an obvious reason to.

Boiled Water is Safe to Drink

Boiled water does not always mean pure water. While much of the germs in water could be killed after boiling, it could have been contaminated by fuel or unknown chemicals in the first place. If you are unsure about the water's source, it may be safer to drink bottled water from your supplies. Nevertheless, boiling is still useful if you are obtaining water in the wild. If you are unable to boil water, you could use filters and disinfectants to purify it.

Chapter 17: Food Dehydration

Dehydrating your own food is a lot like home canning. It is an excellent way to preserve your excess fresh food. Dehydrated food will last years when stored properly. The process is fairly simple and requires almost no training. However, experience and practice will certainly yield better outcomes as you get the hang of drying times and spice needs.

Dehydration is the process of removing as much moisture from a food as possible. Dehydrated food can be eaten as is or soaked in water to return to its normal state. You can add spices or sweeteners to food before you dehydrate it to give it a little more flavor. The drying process does zap out some of the original flavor. It also removes a great deal of the vitamins and nutritional value of the food.

A food dehydrator is a fairly inexpensive piece of equipment that you are sure to get a lot of use out of. You can find plenty of used dehydrators, but unless you know for sure the thing works effectively, you are better off making the investment in a new one.

Check out all of the items you can put in the dehydrator and add to your stockpile.

Thinly sliced meats

Fruits; apples, oranges, strawberries

Vegetables; corn, potatoes, green beans

Herbs; oregano, cilantro, dill, mint and so on

Dehydrated foods are an ideal way to store food for long term because they do not require a lot of room. Using a vacuum sealer helps compact the food while keeping it fresh. Unlike the glass jars of home canning, the bags of dehydrated food can be tossed about without fear of being broken. They are also a lot lighter.

To store dehydrated food, you want to keep it as dry as possible. Silica gel packs are great for tossing in with your dehydrated foods to absorb any oxygen that may be in the food. Oxygen means moisture, which is the number one enemy of dried foods.

You can store your dried foods in jars if you desire. Seal the jars with a lid and band. Typically, the jars will seal within 12 to 24 hours. Another option is to seal the food in Mylar bags. Store the Mylar bags as they are or seal them in food grade buckets.

Check for signs of moisture often. If you notice any condensation on the inside of the bag, you will need to reopen the bag and allow the food to dry a bit more. If you notice any mold on the food, it is necessary to throw the food out. It cannot be saved.

As you get more practice with the drying process, you will be able to determine when food is dry enough to be put in storage. Food that is easily bent or feels damp is not ready to be stored. Of course, on the other end of things, food that snaps or crumbles is too dry and is not going to store well.

Conclusion

By now, you may have already realized that prepping your survival pantry is like an investment. For the most part, it takes time, effort and money to properly supply your pantry and keep a complete set of tools. You'll need to properly strategize your purchases and maximize the space in your pantry. You will need to strengthen your home to protect your family from natural calamities and unwanted intruders.

But other than these, what you'll need is a strong spirit. When disaster itself strikes, you'll need presence of mind, alertness and resourcefulness to keep your family alive and safe from harm. Most of all, there must be full cooperation within the family in order to keep the spirits up and to keep each other safe from harm. Better yet, hold a family meeting to discuss emergency plans and actions at least once a year. Teach your kids the values of disaster preparedness, vigilance and resourcefulness so that even at an early age, they may be able to make right decisions on their own. Keep yourself updated with the latest news so that you won't miss out on news of predicted natural calamities like storms and blizzards. You don't have to be a good scout to be constantly well prepared.

After a disaster, cleaning up your homes and fixing anything that may be broken is important to keep your house safe and suitable for living. Refill your survival pantry, remembering the guidelines set in this book. Finally, don't forget to lend a helping hand to the rest of the community. Encourage everyone to emerge stronger and more prepared for the next disaster that may come.